# English Result

## Pre-intermediate Workbook

Joe McKenna

OXFORD
UNIVERSITY PRESS

# How to talk about names

**G** possessive *'s* **V** family; parts of names

**1A**

## A Vocabulary family

**1** Find all the family words in the pyramid and write them below.

f a
t h e r d a
u g h t e r h u
s b a n d s i s t e r u
n c l e g r a n d m o t h e
r c o u s i n g r a n d f a t h e r a u
n t b r o t h e r w i f e s o n m o t h e r

*uncle* ________ ________
________ ________
________ ________
________ ________
________ ________
________ ________
________

## B Grammar possessive *'s*

**2** Underline the correct word in the sentences.

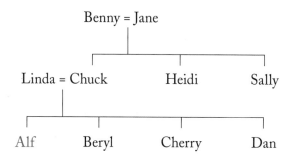

Benny = Jane
Linda = Chuck    Heidi    Sally
Alf    Beryl    Cherry    Dan

1 Alf's grandmother's / grandmothers' name is Jane.
2 His sister's / sisters' names are Beryl and Cherry.
3 His father's / fathers' name is Chuck.
4 His aunt's / aunts' names are Heidi and Sally.
5 His brother's / brothers' name is Dan.
6 His grandfather's / grandfathers' name is Benny.

## C Vocabulary parts of names

**3** Read about John Wayne and complete the sentences with these words.

first name   middle name   nickname
surname   ~~stage name~~

**John Wayne**

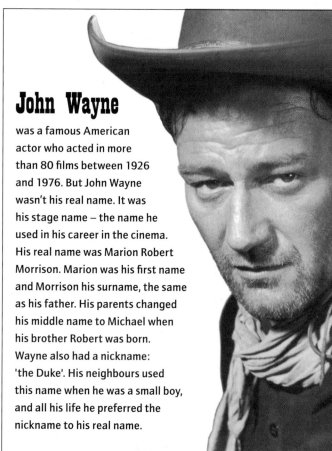

was a famous American actor who acted in more than 80 films between 1926 and 1976. But John Wayne wasn't his real name. It was his stage name – the name he used in his career in the cinema. His real name was Marion Robert Morrison. Marion was his first name and Morrison his surname, the same as his father. His parents changed his middle name to Michael when his brother Robert was born. Wayne also had a nickname: 'the Duke'. His neighbours used this name when he was a small boy, and all his life he preferred the nickname to his real name.

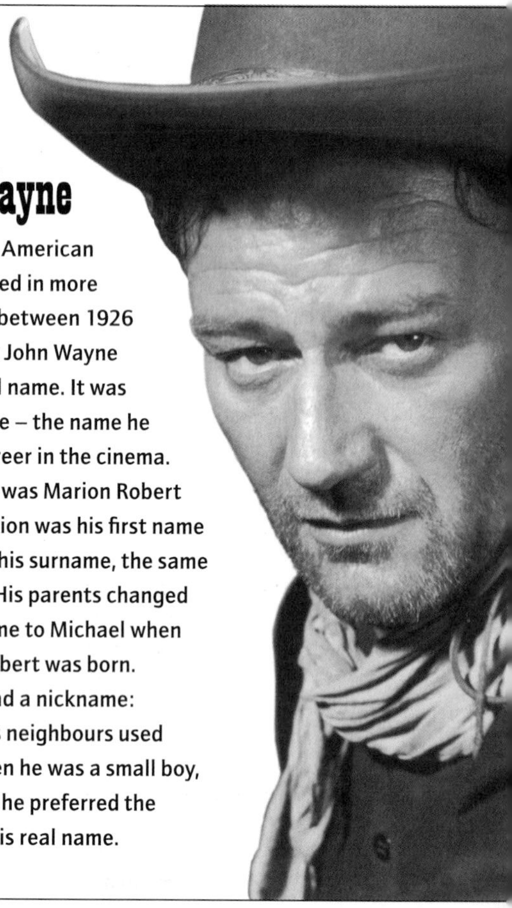

1 John Wayne was his *stage name*.
2 Marion was his ________.
3 Morrison was his ________.
4 Michael was his ________.
5 The Duke was his ________.

| **And you?** Answer the questions. |
|---|
| 1 How many names have you got? |
| 2 Who chose your name(s)? |
| 3 Do you like your name(s)? |
| 4 Imagine you have two children – a boy and a girl. Write three names you like and three you don't like. |

How well can you talk about names now?
Go back to the Student's Book >> p.7 and tick ✓ the line again.

# How to give and understand personal details

**G** present simple -*s* or -*es* ending **V** documents and personal details **P** when is -*s* an extra syllable?

1B

## A Vocabulary documents and personal details

**1** Complete the crossword.

**Across**

2 A little book you need when you travel to a different country.
4 To post something, put a stamp on this, and write the name and address on the front.
7 A document that shows that you can drive.
8 You wear it on your jacket. It says you are part of a special group.

**Down**

1 A small piece of paper with a message.
3 A piece of plastic you can use if you don't have cash.
5 You need this when you travel by bus, train, or plane.
6 The traditional way of writing to people on paper.

**2** Complete the form with the correct details.

Wilfred Winterbottom was born in Chester, England 71 years ago. He's retired now and he spends all his time travelling. He travels to places that you and I can't visit because we don't have the time or the money. He travels so much that he doesn't have a normal home. He doesn't have a phone either because he normally communicates by letter. It's easy to see why he isn't married and has no children. 'I never had time to meet the right person – and I never stay in the same place anyway!' he says. He collects hats from all the places he visits, and he learns a new language every year.

Surname: *Winterbottom*
First name: ____________
Age: ____________
Nationality: ____________
Place of birth: ____________
Marital status: ____________
Job: ____________
Interests: ____________

## B Grammar present simple -*s* or -*es* ending

**3** Add -*s* or -*es* to the verbs in the text.

Tom Klutz is an artist. Well, he [1]think *s* ______ he's an artist. He [2]go ______ to art school in the morning, when he [3]remember ______ to. He [4]miss ______ a lot of classes because he [5]sleep ______ late. He [6]sleep ______ late because he [7]talk ______ and [8]drink ______ and [9]dance ______ until late. He also [10]watch ______ art documentaries and [11]make ______ notes and plans for the future. You're probably thinking: when [12]do ______ he actually paint? He [13]say ______ he [14]paint ______ when he [15]feel ______ like it. We didn't ask him to explain.

## C Pronunciation when is -*s* an extra syllable?

**4** Do these pairs of sentences have the same or different numbers of syllables? Write *S* for *same* or *D* for *different*.

1 I eat and drink. She eats and drinks. *S*
2 You teach and watch. She teaches and watches. ____
3 We sit and think. He sits and thinks. ____
4 They paint and draw. He paints and draws. ____
5 I push and close. She pushes and closes. ____
6 We play and sing. He plays and sings. ____
7 You kiss and dance. She kisses and dances. ____
8 They wash and finish. He washes and finishes. ____

**5** **1B.1▸** Listen and check.

**6** In the second sentences, underline the verbs where -*s* is an extra syllable.

**7** Listen again and repeat.

How well can you give and understand personal details now?
Go back to the Student's Book >> p.9 and tick ✓ the line again.

# How to ask questions about people

**G** *be* and *do* in questions **V** question pronouns **P** rhythm in *Wh-* questions

1C

## A Vocabulary question pronouns

**1** Complete the policeman's questions with these words.
what who how where

1 *What* is your name?
2 ________ are you from?
3 ________ do you do?
4 ________ were you last night?
5 ________ were you with?
6 ________ often do you go there?
7 ________ did you go after that?
8 ________ time did you arrive home?

**2** Match the questions in exercise 1 with the answers.
a ☐ I'm a teacher.
b [1] Maria Turner.
c ☐ London.
d ☐ Some friends.
e ☐ Once or twice a month.
f ☐ At the Jazz Bar.
g ☐ Sometime after midnight.
h ☐ To my friend's flat.

## B Grammar *be* and *do* in questions

**3** Put the verb(s) in brackets in the sentences.
1 Where *are* my glasses? On your head! (are)
2 What he doing? He reading. ('s, 's)
3 What he do? He a taxi driver. (does, 's)
4 Where you live? Near the station. (do)
5 Why you crying? Because I very unhappy! (are, 'm)
6 How this work? Push the red button. (does)
7 When you finish school? Six years ago. (did)
8 Who you talk to on the phone? My sister. (did)
9 Why Tony get divorced? I know! (did, don't)
10 What Ibiza like? It wonderful! (was, was)

## C Pronunciation rhythm in *Wh-* questions

**4** 1C.1▶ Read and listen.

| ● | • | • | ● |
|---|---|---|---|
| Why | is | he | late? |
| Where | is | he | now? |
| What | did | he | do? |
| What | did | he | say? |
| When | did | he | leave? |
| Who | was | he | with? |
| What | was | she | like? |
| Where | did | they | go? |

**5** Listen again and repeat. Copy the rhythm.

**And you?** Imagine you went out last night. Answer the questions from exercise 1.

1
2
3
4
5
6
7
8



How well can you ask questions about people now?
Go back to the Student's Book >> p.11 and tick ✓ the line again.

# How to talk about vocabulary

# 1D

**G** grammar in the dictionary **V** definition words **P** pronunciation in the dictionary

## A Grammar in the dictionary

**1** Match the underlined words with the definitions.

1 [b] Have you got any matches?
2 ☐ What kind of leaf is that?
3 ☐ Do you eat meat?
4 ☐ He bought a newspaper.
5 ☐ That's a nice ring!
6 ☐ A new white dress.
7 ☐ Turn right!
8 ☐ They left at 9.30.
9 ☐ He stood up very slowly.
10 ☐ I think he's a very strange person.

a An adjective. The opposite of 'black'.
b ~~A plural noun. We use these to make fire.~~
c A noun. Married people often have one on their finger.
d A past tense verb. It means the same as 'go away'.
e An adverb. The opposite of 'fast'.
f A noun. A kind of food which comes from animals.
g A past tense verb. To take something for money.
h An adjective. The opposite of 'normal'.
i An adverb. It tells you which way to go.
j A noun. You can see this on trees and plants.

## B Vocabulary definition words

**2** Complete the definitions with these words.

kind means opposite past sounds

1 **Son** *sounds* the same as **sun**.
2 **Right** is the ________ of **left**.
3 **Bought** is the ________ of **buy**.
4 **Small** ________ the same as **little**.
5 **Arrived** is the ________ of **left**.
6 **Chicken** is a ________ of **meat**.
7 **Right** ________ the same as **write**.
8 **Went** is the ________ of **go**.
9 **Big** is the ________ of **small**.

**3** Write definitions for the underlined words. Use the words in brackets.

1 Can I see your passport? (sounds)
*See sounds the same as sea*.
2 This shop is closed. Please ring again later. (means)
________.
3 He's got long hair and glasses. (opposite)
________.
4 She wrote him a long letter. (past)
________.
5 I'll have the salmon, please. (kind)
________.
6 Nice to meet you. (sounds)
________.

## C Pronunciation in the dictionary

**4** Match the words that sound the same. Check the pronunciation in your dictionary.

| | |
|---|---|
| 1 [b] quay | a flour /ˈflaʊə/ |
| 2 ☐ eight | b ~~key /kiː/~~ |
| 3 ☐ blue | c nose /nəʊz/ |
| 4 ☐ knows | d wear /weə/ |
| 5 ☐ flower | e bored /bɔːd/ |
| 6 ☐ wood | f ate /eɪt/ |
| 7 ☐ guessed | g blew /bluː/ |
| 8 ☐ where | h would /wʊd/ |
| 9 ☐ board | i guest /gest/ |

**5** 1D.1 ▸ Listen and check.

**6** Listen again and repeat.

How well can you talk about vocabulary now?
Go back to the Student's Book >> p.13 and tick ✓ the line again.

# Unit 1 Skills Practice

## A Read for key words

1 Read the text and complete the sentences with these names.
Sulaemi Eddy ~~Suryono~~ Indrawan Gunawan Indrawati Paulus Susi

In Java, there's no tradition of surnames or family names. Javanese people in general have only one name, for example Suryono or Gunawan. The ending often shows gender, so Indrawan is used for a man, and Indrawati for a woman.

Most names come from the Javanese language, but there are other kinds of name, too. Many names come from Arabic, so you often find people with two names, like Zainil Arifin or Sulaemi Ma'ruf. There are also Christian names from colonial times, and they are often in Latin – Paulus, for example.

Finally, it's becoming more common now to use a western first name together with a traditional Javanese name, for example Eddy Hermanto or Susi Pramono. When you speak to Javanese or other Indonesians, it's important to ask which name they prefer to use.

1 *Suryono* and ________ are typical Javanese names.
2 ________ is a female name, and ________ is a male name.
3 ________ is a name that comes from Arabic.
4 ________ is a Christian name.
5 ________ and ________ are names that are becoming more popular.

2 It is a good idea to start a vocabulary notebook for recording new words. Write the word, the part of speech, and an example sentence. Choose four words from the Java text to start your notebook.

| *word* | *part of speech* | *example sentence* |
|---|---|---|
| *tradition* | *noun* | *In Poland, it's a tradition to give Christmas presents on Christmas Eve.* |
| | | |
| | | |

## B Listen and understand

3 1S.1▸ A man and a woman meet on the train. Listen to their conversation. Write *M* for man and *W* for woman.

1 Who is going to Sheffield? *M, W*
2 Who doesn't live in Sheffield? ________
3 Who is an artist? ________
4 Who is going to a meeting in Sheffield? ________
5 Who is a police officer? ________

4 Listen and put the phrases in the order you hear them.
a [*1*] And you?
b [ ] Oh!
c [ ] Me?
d [ ] Not exactly.
e [ ] That's interesting!
f [ ] Oh really?
g [ ] I see.
h [ ] Is that right?

5 Listen again and complete the sentences.
**B** I'm going there, too.
**A** Do you ________ there?
**B** No, I'm just visiting. I've got some ________ there.
**A** Oh really? ________ do you do?
**B** I'm an artist.
**A** That's interesting! ________ you paint pictures of ________?

6 Check the audio script on >> p.91.

## C Read personal information

**7** Read the text quickly and match the headings with the paragraphs.

My studies   My job   My family   My free time

1 ____________

I have five brothers and sisters, and I'm number two. When we were young, it was fun living with a lot of people, but sometimes it could be a problem. I often lost my things, and I always had to wait for my turn to use the bathroom. But the house was always full, and there was always lots to do.

2 ____________

In general, I enjoy my work. I'm an assistant in a theatre, so I usually work in the evenings, and especially at weekends. I meet a lot of interesting people – and I don't have to pay for tickets! But my girlfriend would like us to go out more together at weekends.

3 ____________

I go to language classes in the morning. Many of the other students work in the evenings, so we have a lot in common. I study English because I want to travel and talk to people.

4 ____________

I read a lot and I also play the guitar. At the weekend, I meet some friends and we go cycling together. If the weather's bad, we go and play music or watch a film at a friend's house. I don't play sports and I don't like football very much.

**8** Which words helped you in exercise 7? Underline them in the text.

**9** Read the text again more carefully. Write *true* or *false*.

1 He's the oldest of his brothers and sisters. *False*
2 He works at weekends. ____________
3 He and his girlfriend often go out at weekends. ____________
4 He studies English in the morning. ____________
5 He likes cycling on his own. ____________
6 He enjoys watching football. ____________

## D Write about a person you met recently

**10** Complete the text with these phrases.

come to class   the other day   reads it too   every year   for work

*I met an interesting person in class 1____________. I mean, I knew her name, but we never had a conversation before. Her name's Sonia. She's French, like all of us, but her mother's Russian. I didn't know that! So she speaks Russian, and 2____________, but she doesn't write it very well. She's studying English because she needs it 3____________. She also plays the violin in an orchestra and travels round Europe 4____________. That's why sometimes she doesn't 5____________. You never know who you're going to meet!*

**11** Read the text and correct six more spelling mistakes.

The other day, I was talking to Jean-Jacques. He's the same age as me, but he's got a ~~jobe~~ *job*. He works in a factori in a different part of town. He says the job isn't very interesting, but he gets eneuf money to pay for a small car. He loves taking fotographs and he knows a lot about it. He spends a lot of his free time wisiting new places and taking pictures. Maybe he can help me with my knew digital camra.

**12** Write five or six sentences about someone you met recently. Check your spelling when you finish.

____________
____________
____________
____________
____________
____________

**Now try the Self check on** >> p.76.

# How to ask for tourist information

**v** tourist attractions   **P** rhythm in *How* questions

## A Vocabulary tourist attractions

1   Write the names of the places.

| | | |
|---|---|---|
| 1 d*esert* | 5 c_____ | 9 r_____ |
| 2 m_____ | 6 l_____ | 10 b_____ |
| 3 f_____ | 7 r_____ | 11 c_____ |
| 4 v_____ | 8 r_____ | 12 i_____ |

## B Pronunciation rhythm in *How* questions

2   Complete the questions with these words.

old   much   long   high   far

● ●

1   How _____ is it?

● ●

2   How _____ is it?

● ●

3   How _____ is it?

● ●

4   How _____ are they?

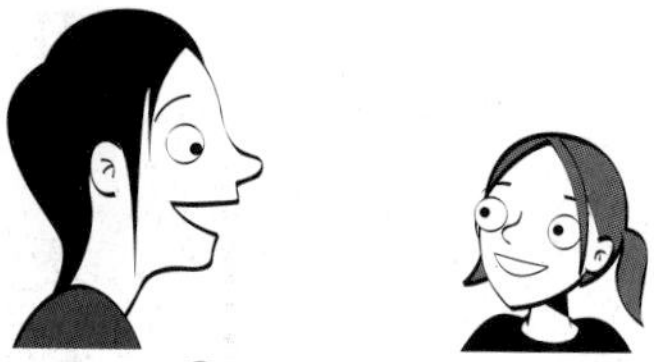

● ●

5   How _____ are you?

3   **2A.1▶** Listen and check.

4   Listen again and repeat the questions.

How well can you ask for tourist information now?
Go back to the Student's Book >> p.17 and tick ✓ the line again.

# How to describe places

**2B**

**G** adjective order **V** fact and opinion adjectives **P** stress-timed rhythm

## A Vocabulary fact and opinion adjectives

**1** Put these adjectives in the correct box.

~~lovely~~ quiet green pretty beautiful old white warm little interesting grey high new nice blue

| opinion | fact |
|---|---|
| *lovely* | |

**2** Complete the sentences with opposite adjectives from exercise 1.

1 It's a really *beautiful* (ugly) city.
2 London is quite ________ (cool) in July.
3 The church was lovely and ________ (noisy).
4 New York has lots of ________ (low) buildings.
5 This is probably the most ________ (boring) part of the country.
6 There's a ________ (horrible) little café in the town.

## B Grammar adjective order

**3** Put the phrases in order.

**The North of Spain**

1 little pretty villages
*pretty little villages*
2 colourful forests fine
________
3 mountains cloud-covered beautiful
________
4 old churches interesting
________
5 rivers lovely cool
________

**The West of Scotland**

6 lighthouses white pretty
________
7 islands green lovely
________
8 clean beaches nice
________
9 towns little fine
________
10 ruins old interesting
________

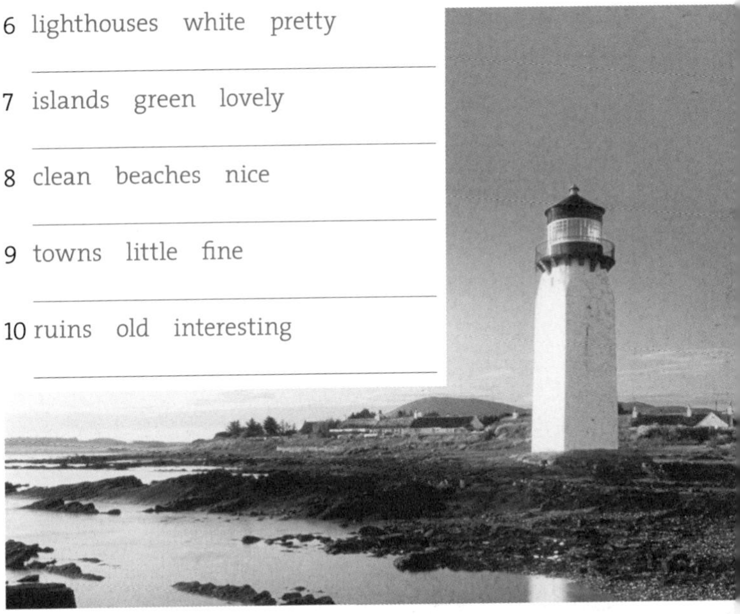

## C Pronunciation stress-timed rhythm

**4** **2B.1▸** Listen to the rhythm in the phrases. Write *a*, *b*, or *c*.

a = ● ● ●
b = ●• ●• ●•
c = ●•• ●•• ●••

1 [*b*] lovely quiet beaches
2 [ ] wonderful tropical rainforests
3 [ ] cool clear lakes
4 [ ] pretty mountain railways
5 [ ] nice old towns
6 [ ] noisy little markets

**5** Listen again and repeat.

**And you?** Translate the phrases in exercise 3. Is the word order the same in your language?

| |
|---|
| 1 |
| 2 |
| 3 |
| 4 |
| 5 |
| 6 |
| 7 |
| 8 |
| 9 |
| 10 |

How well can you describe places now?
Go back to the Student's Book >> p.19 and tick ✓ the line again.

# How to compare the weather in different places

# 2C

**G** comparative and superlative adjectives **V** weather **P** *-er* and *-est* endings

## A Vocabulary weather

**1** Find ten weather words in the puzzle.

| | | | | | | | |
|---|---|---|---|---|---|---|---|
| E | T | Y | H | S | N | O | W |
| H | (C | L | O | U | D | Y) | I |
| S | O | X | T | N | Y | W | N |
| T | L | I | P | N | O | L | D |
| O | D | Q | R | Y | I | K | Y |
| R | F | R | A | I | N | N | A |
| M | W | A | R | M | J | H | U |
| V | M | A | Z | M | F | O | G |

**2** Complete the sentences with these weather words.

high light rain lowest ~~hottest~~ wettest heavy

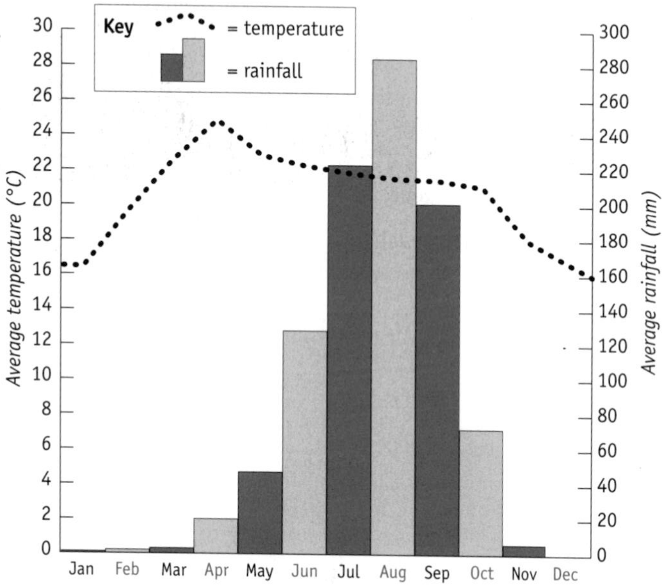


1 April is the *hottest* month.
2 It doesn't ________ in December.
3 The ________ temperatures are from November to January.
4 August is the ________ month.
5 From November to March there is only ________ rainfall.
6 The average temperatures aren't very ________.
7 There is ________ rainfall from July to September.

## B Grammar comparative and superlative adjectives

**3** Complete the sentences using the information in the chart.

| | Beijing (China) | Bergen (Norway) | Buenos Aires (Argentina) |
|---|---|---|---|
| **June** | | | |
| Average temperature (°C) | 24.4 | 16 | 10.4 |
| Average rainfall (mm) | 76 | 126 | 64 |

1 *Beijing* is 14° *hotter* than Buenos Aires. (hot)
2 ________ is the ________ city in June. (cool)
3 ________ is the ________ city in June. (hot)
4 Bergen is ________ than ________. (warm)
5 Beijing is ________ than ________. (wet)
6 ________ has the ________ rainfall in June. (heavy)
7 ________ has the ________ rainfall in June. (light)
8 ________ has the ________ temperature in June. (high)

## C Pronunciation *-er* and *-est* endings

**4** **2C.1▸** Listen and underline the words you hear.

1 warm / warmer / warmest
2 heavy / heavier / heaviest
3 high / higher / highest
4 uncomfortable / more uncomfortable / most uncomfortable
5 wet / wetter / wettest
6 good / better / best

**5** Listen again and repeat the phrases.

**And you?** Write about the weather where you live.

In December, *it's cold and we often have snow*.
In January, ________.
In March, ________.
In May, ________.
In July, ________.
In September, ________.
In November, ________.

How well can you compare the weather in different places now?
Go back to the Student's Book >> p.21 and tick ✓ the line again.

# How to talk about personal things

**G** past simple **V** souvenirs, countries, and regions



## A Vocabulary souvenirs, countries, and regions

**1** Complete the puzzle. What is the word in grey?

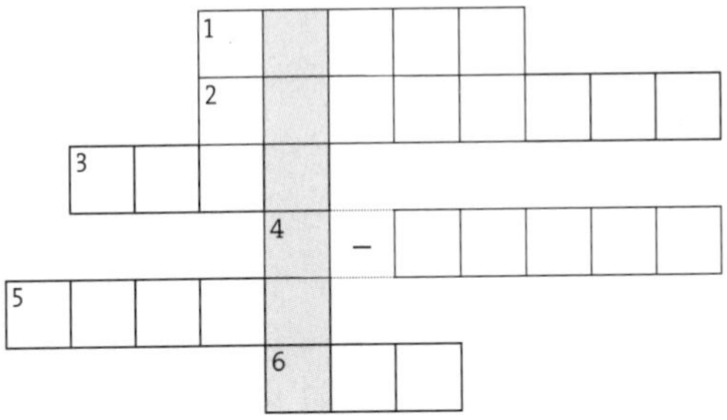

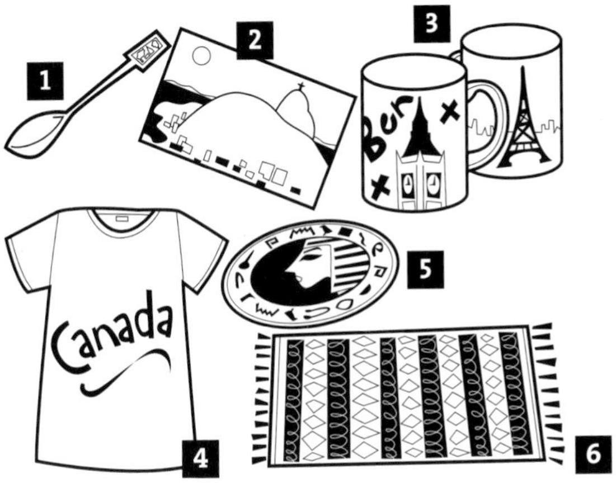


**2** Match these countries with the descriptions.

Austria China Egypt Greece ~~Panama~~ Peru Tunisia

1 In Central America. It's between Costa Rica and Colombia.
*Panama*

2 In South America. It's west of Bolivia and Brazil.
_______

3 In North Africa. It's south of Italy.
_______

4 In north-east Africa. It's near Jordan.
_______

5 In Asia. It's between India and Japan.
_______

6 In central Europe. It's south of Germany.
_______

7 In southern Europe. It's between Italy and Turkey.
_______

## B Grammar past simple

**3** Complete the text with the past simple form of these verbs.

buy ~~get~~ not go love not have leave bring take

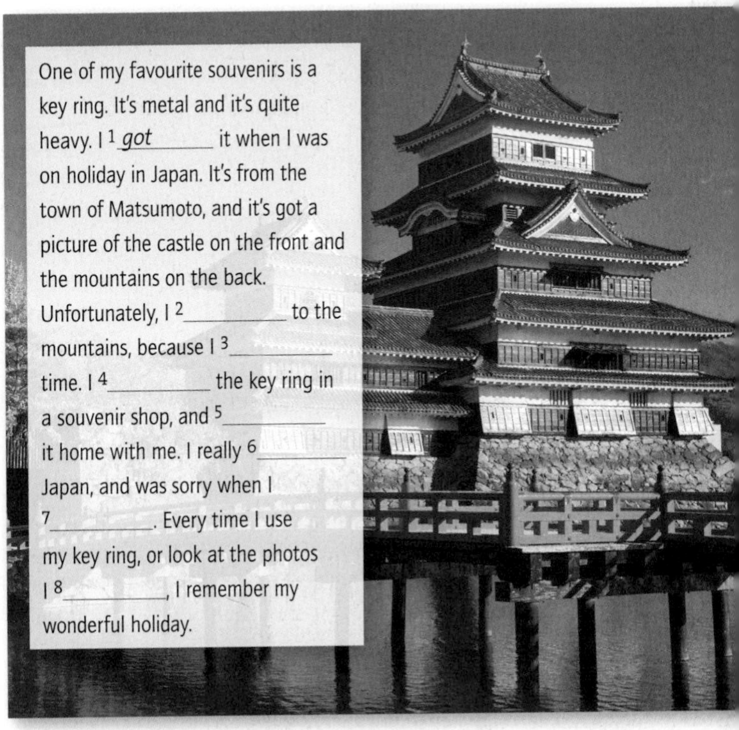

One of my favourite souvenirs is a key ring. It's metal and it's quite heavy. I [1] *got* it when I was on holiday in Japan. It's from the town of Matsumoto, and it's got a picture of the castle on the front and the mountains on the back. Unfortunately, I [2] _______ to the mountains, because I [3] _______ time. I [4] _______ the key ring in a souvenir shop, and [5] _______ it home with me. I really [6] _______ Japan, and was sorry when I [7] _______. Every time I use my key ring, or look at the photos I [8] _______, I remember my wonderful holiday.

**4** Put the questions in order.

1 rug where that you get did
*Where did you get that rug*?

2 it buy where she did
_______?

3 Morocco go when she to did
_______?

4 there she it did like
_______?

5 travel how she did
_______?

6 desert visit she the did
_______?

**5** Match the questions in exercise 4 with the answers.

a [3] About three years ago.
b ☐ By train, ferry, and bus.
c ☐ It was a present from my sister.
d ☐ No, because she didn't have time.
e ☐ She said it was great.
f ☐ In Morocco.

**How well can you talk about personal things now?**
Go back to the Student's Book >> p.23 and tick ✓ the line again.

# Unit 2 Skills Practice

## A Listen for key information

**1** 2S.1▶ Listen to two people talking about the weather in Mexico. Who are they?

a a professor and a student
b a tourist and a travel agent

**2** Now listen again and underline the correct answer.

1 The dry season is November–June / June–November.
2 The capital is cooler in the morning / afternoon.
3 Temperatures on the coast are higher / lower than inland.
4 Temperatures at the ruins are higher / lower than on the coast.
5 In Yucatan, rainfall is higher / lower than in the capital.

**3** Listen again and put these key phrases in the order you hear them.

a ☐ much more rain
b [1] two different seasons
c ☐ the best time to travel
d ☐ from June to November
e ☐ the wettest months

## B Read for key words

**4** Match the headings with the paragraphs.

Back to nature  Explore the past  On your own two feet  Sun, sea, and sand

### Visit Mexico!

**THERE ARE SO MANY KINDS OF ACTIVITIES FOR TOURISTS VISITING MEXICO. IT ALL DEPENDS ON WHAT YOU LIKE DOING.**

1 ______________________ Why not relax on some of the best beaches in the world? Cancun and Acapulco offer beautiful tropical beaches which are visited by thousands of tourists every year. Foreign visitors love the warm, sunny weather and brilliant blue skies.

2 ______________________ Maybe you prefer a more active holiday, for example walking in the mountains of the Sierra Madre. The weather there is cooler, and the views are spectacular. You can also visit Indian villages which have not changed much since the Spanish arrived in the 16th century. If you feel really energetic, you can climb a big, snow-capped volcano. At 5,452 metres above sea level, Popocatépetl is the highest mountain in Mexico, and forms part of the Izt-Popo National Park.

3 ______________________ Are you tired of cities and traffic? There are almost one hundred national parks in Mexico, from hot deserts in the north, to cool rainforests in the mountains, and tropical forests in the east. You can see hundreds of amazing plants and animals in their natural habitats.

4 ______________________ Do you like learning when you're on holiday? Mexico is well-known for its rich Aztec and Maya history. There are many important ancient ruins, for example Teotihuacán and Chichén Itzá, with their impressive temples where people went to pray. There are also many fine national and regional museums to visit.

**SO YOU SEE, THERE IS SOMETHING FOR EVERYONE IN MEXICO!**

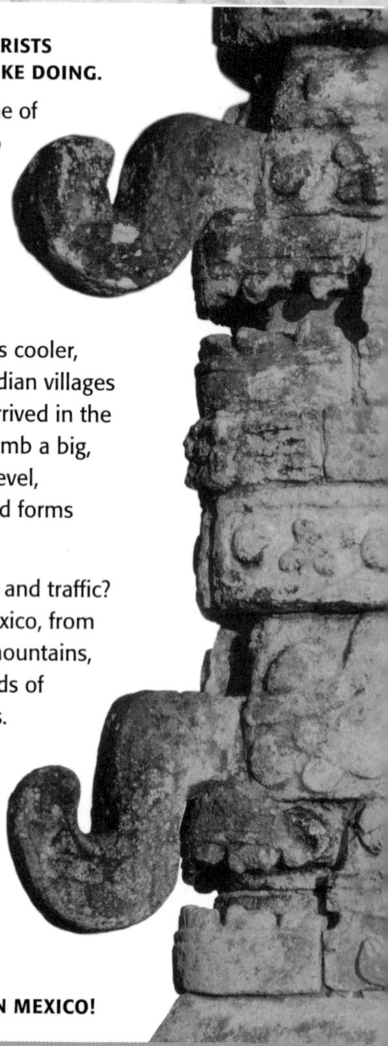

**5** Write one example of these from the text.

1 a beach ______________
2 a mountain ______________
3 a national park ______________
4 ancient ruins ______________

**6** You can find out how to pronounce new words by looking in your dictionary. For example, this mark (ˈ) comes before the stressed syllable. Use your dictionary to find the meaning and pronunciation of the highlighted words in the text.

**century** /ˈsentʃəri/ *n* (*pl* **centuries**) **1** siglo **2** (*críquet*) cien carreras

*Diccionario Oxford Pocket para estudiantes de inglés*

## C Read for detail

**7** Read the text and complete the table.

### CLASSIC TRAIN JOURNEYS:
# THE COPPER CANYON EXPRESS

**One of the most exciting train journeys in the world is the Copper Canyon Express in Mexico. The train travels from the state capital of Chihuahua inland, through the western Sierra Madre mountains, and down to the town of Los Mochis on the Pacific coast. It's a scenic trip you'll never forget.**

Let me give you some facts and figures about this railway line. It took 63 years to build, is 941 km long, and has a total of 410 bridges. That means approximately one bridge every two kilometres! And at its highest point, the train travels at 2,450 metres above sea level.

The whole trip takes about 16 hours, but most people stay overnight in one of the towns along the way. Many travellers stay in Posada Barrancas to enjoy the spectacular views of the canyon.

The train service runs all year round, both in the dry season and in the wet season. If you're travelling between November and February, you might find snow. Between March and June, it's hot and dry and there are often forest fires. Perhaps the best time to make the trip is in September, near the end of the wet season. The temperatures are warmer, the scenery is greener, and you can hear the rivers and see the waterfalls.

### COPPER CANYON EXPRESS

Started 1861 – finished [1] ___________

Length [2] ___________ km

Bridges [3] ___________

Maximum height above sea level [4] ___________ m

Journey time [5] ___________

Best time to go [6] ___________

**8** Choose five words you do not know in the text and guess their meanings. Try these strategies to help you.
- Decide if it is a verb, noun, adjective, etc.
- Think about similar words in your language.
- Look at the other words in the sentence.

**9** Now check the words in your dictionary. Which strategy helped the most?

## D Write about a place you would like to visit

**10** Complete the text with these phrases.

very cold   outdoor holiday   long holidays   spectacular scenery

One of the places I would most like to visit is New Zealand, especially the South Island. I think it would be wonderful for an [1] ___________. There are snow-covered mountains, beautiful rainforests, amazing hiking routes, and [2] ___________. Do you remember the films of *The Lord of the Rings*? They used many locations in New Zealand.

New Zealand would be a good place to visit because I can practise my English there. Also, I live in Sweden, where it's [3] ___________ in winter. I always have [4] ___________ at Christmas, so I can visit New Zealand when it's summer there.

**11** Think about a place you would like to visit. What adjectives can you use to describe the scenery, weather, etc.?

**Example** wonderful old castles

**12** Write about a place you would like to visit. Describe the place and explain why you want to go there.

___________________________________________

___________________________________________

___________________________________________

___________________________________________

___________________________________________

___________________________________________

___________________________________________

___________________________________________

Now try the Self check on >> p.77.

# How to talk about likes and dislikes

**G** *like doing; would like to do* **V** adventure sports **P** consonant clusters

# 3A

## A Vocabulary adventure sports

**1** Complete the names of the sports.

1 s*kiing*______

2 w__________

3 s__________

4 s__________

5 w__________

6 s__________

7 d__________

8 c__________

9 r__________
s__________

10 s__________-
__________

## B Grammar *like doing; would like to do*

**2** Underline the correct answer.

1 I can't drive, but I would like learn / to learn.
2 We like swim / swimming in the pool at midnight!
3 What do you like do / doing on holiday?
4 She says she wouldn't like trying / to try snowboarding.
5 I'd like find / to find a solution to the problem.
6 My children don't like sleep / sleeping in the dark.
7 Would you like going / to go away for the weekend?
8 He doesn't like do / doing the housework.

**3** Underline the correct words.

**Julie** I like most water sports, so [1] I like swimming/ I'd like to swim and I also [2] like surfing / would like to surf. I'm a really good surfer. [3] I love trying / I'd love to try scuba-diving too, because it looks like a lot of fun!

**Rob** I prefer windsurfing and waterskiing. They're much more exciting. When I'm on holiday, I [4] love going / would love to go waterskiing every day. If it's windy, then [5] I like going / I'd like to go windsurfing. There isn't any scuba-diving at our beach, but [6] I love trying / I'd love to try it some time.

**Ellie** I don't live near the water, so my sports are mountain sports. [7] I love climbing / I'd love to climb. We go climbing twice a month and spend the weekend outdoors. In winter [8] I like skiing / I'd like to ski, because there's a lot of snow. I'm getting better every year. My brother says I should go ice-climbing with him, and [9] I like trying / I'd like to try it.

## C Pronunciation consonant clusters

**4** Underline the words beginning with *sn-*, *sp-*, *sk-*, *st-*, and *sm-*.

1 I saw a snake in the street.
2 There's a spider on the stairs.
3 My skateboard's at school.
4 Steve is standing at the bus stop.
5 The small boy is smiling.

**5** **3A.1▶** Listen and copy the pronunciation.

| **And you?** Write: |
|---|
| two activities you like doing. |
| two activities you'd like to try. |
| two activities you wouldn't like to try. |

**How well can you talk about likes and dislikes now?**
Go back to the Student's Book >> p.27 and tick ✓ the line again.

# How to talk about your abilities

**G** ability **V** abilities **P** stressing the negative

3B

## A Vocabulary abilities

**1** Complete the sentences with these verbs.

do use ~~read~~ make play read ride use

1 I can *read* Chinese and Arabic, but I can't ________ your handwriting!
2 My sisters ________ basketball very well and they also ________ their own clothes.
3 Can you ________ a sewing machine? Wow! I wish I could.
4 Which is easier to ________: a horse or a camel?
5 I often ________ crosswords, but my wife prefers sudokus.
6 Can you help me? I don't know how to ________ this camera.

## B Grammar ability

**2** Complete the answers with *can*, *can't*, *could*, or *couldn't*, and these verbs.

cook ~~do~~ find hear play remember sing stop

1 **A** How fast can you type?
**B** I *can do* 70 words a minute.
2 **A** Why were you so late this morning?
**B** I ________ my keys and I missed the bus.
3 **A** Did you enjoy the show?
**B** Absolutely! I ________ laughing!
4 **A** Are you good at sports?
**B** I ________ basketball quite well, but I'm not a very good swimmer.
5 **A** Why didn't you finish the exam?
**B** Because I ________ the answers.
6 **A** What about housework?
**B** Cleaning is not a problem, but I ________.
7 **A** Why did you wake up early?
**B** Because I ________ people downstairs.
8 **A** Are these your opera prizes?
**B** Yes – I ________ quite well when I was younger.

**3** Order the words to make sentences and questions.

1 music was read she five when could
My sister *could read music when she was five*.
2 when jigsaws he was do two
He could ________.
3 you musical a play instrument
Can ________?
4 can't out get I bed of mornings
On Monday ________.
5 bike I six a couldn't ride
When I was ________.
6 map couldn't I read because the
I got lost ________.

## C Pronunciation stressing the negative

**4** Complete the rhyme with these words.

straight eight ~~five~~ drive eight straight

He could dive at *five*
He could skate at ________
But he wasn't able to ________
And he couldn't swim ________
Now he can drive, at twenty-________
But he still can't swim ________

**5** **3B.1▸** Listen and check.

**6** Listen again and copy the pronunciation. Practise stressing the negative.

**How well can you talk about your abilities now?**
Go back to the Student's Book >> p.29 and tick ✓ the line again.

# How to suggest what to do

**3C**

**G** *could* (possibility) **V** making suggestions **P** intonation in suggestions

## A Vocabulary making suggestions

**1** Put the suggestions in order.

1 for shall out a we walk go
*Shall we go out for a walk* ?

2 chess a about game how of
______________________________?

3 in a for pool let's the swim go
______________________________!

4 game play could we a video
______________________________.

5 drink a about to how pub for going the
______________________________?

**2** Match the answers with the suggestions in exercise 1.

a ☐ No, thanks! I don't want to see another TV screen!
b ☐ But it's only eleven o'clock in the morning!
c *1* It's too hot outside.
d ☐ No, I lost three games the last time we played!
e ☐ OK! Let's get some towels.

## B Pronunciation intonation in suggestions

**3** 3C.1▶ Listen to the suggestions in exercise 1. Practise saying the suggestions, and copy the intonation.

## C Grammar *could* (possibility)

**4** Read the story. Look at the examples of *could* and *couldn't*. Write *S* for suggestion or *A* for ability.

**The Birthday Present**

It was my son's birthday and I was worried about it. He was just 13 and I [1]*couldn't decide* what to buy him. I asked the girl in the shop for help. 'You [2]*could buy* him some music,' she said. But I [3]*couldn't do* that because I didn't know what music he liked. The shop assistant said, 'You [4]*could try* this book – it sells very well.' 'OK, I'll take it,' I said. When I gave him the book, he [5]*couldn't wait* to open it, and the smile on his face was real. Finally, I [6]*could relax.*

1 *A*　　3 ______　　5 ______
2 ______　　4 ______　　6 ______

**5** Complete the conversation with *could* and these verbs.

walk run ~~call~~ go back stop

**A** Oh no! What do we do now?
**B** We [1] *could call* for help.
**A** No, we can't. My phone's at home.
**B** Oh. Well, we [2] ____________ to the next town.
**A** It's 40 km! That's too far to walk!
**B** We [3] ____________ another car and ask for help.
**A** The last car went past an hour ago!
**B** OK. We [4] ____________ to that garage we saw on the way here.
**A** I didn't see a garage!
**B** There's one about 20 minutes in that direction.
**A** You [5] ____________ there and get help.
**B** Run? I don't think so!

How well can you suggest what to do now?
Go back to the Student's Book >> p.31 and tick ✓ the line again.

# How to talk about what's going to happen

3D

**G** *going to* (prediction) **V** types of stories; films **P** the letter *r*

## A Vocabulary types of stories; films

**1** Complete the sentences.

1 Bruce Willis often appears in *action* films.
2 A love story is called a ________.
3 The historical film *Cleopatra* is an ________.
4 Shakespeare and Ibsen wrote a lot of ________.
5 Emile Zola wrote many famous ________.
6 A good ________ should make you laugh.
7 *Frankenstein* is a classic ________ movie.
8 ________ ________ films are often set in space.

## B Grammar *going to* (prediction)

**2** Write what is going to happen. Use the verbs in brackets.

1 *He's going to walk into the lamp post*. (he / walk)
2 ________. (it / rain)
3 ________. (the shops / close)
4 ________. (she / buy)

**3** Complete the sentences with the correct form of *going to* and the verbs in brackets.

**A** [1] *Are you going to make* (make) a film with the actor Gary Newman?

**B** I don't know. We [2] ________ (talk) about the possibility this summer.

**A** Some people say you two [3] ________ (get) married.

**B** Let me say very clearly we [4] ________ (not get) married. Gary is a fantastic person to work with, but he [5] ________ (not be) my husband!

**A** [6] ________ (your next film / be) another romance?

**B** Ah, that's a secret! I [7] ________ (not answer) that question. You'll have to wait and see.

**A** [8] ________ (your sister / work) with you?

**B** Er, yes, she'll probably be in my next film.

## C Pronunciation the letter *r*

**4** Look at the description of a film from a TV magazine. Underline the letter *r* when it is NOT pronounced in British English.

**■ RAIDERS OF THE LOST ARK**

The Americans want Doctor Jones to find the famous treasure before it is too late.

*Starring*
HARRISON FORD
KAREN ALLEN
PAUL FREEMAN

**5** 3D.1▸ Listen and check.

**6** Check the audio script on >> p.91.

**7** Listen again and repeat.

| **And you?** Write the name of a film you like. |
|---|
| action film |
| comedy |
| epic |
| romance |
| science fiction |

**How well can you talk about what's going to happen now?**
Go back to the Student's Book >> p.33 and tick ✓ the line again.

# Unit 3 Skills Practice

## A Read for key information

**1** What do you know about skating? Guess the correct answers.

1. Ice skates are about 100 / 1,000 / 5,000 years old.
2. It was the English / French / Dutch who first used skates like the ones we use today.
3. Modern ice skates became popular worldwide in the $17^{th}$ / $18^{th}$ / $19^{th}$ century.
4. Modern roller skates date from the $18^{th}$ / $19^{th}$ / $20^{th}$ century.
5. The first rollerblades were easy / difficult to use.

**2** Read the text and check your answers.

**Ice skates** The idea of skating on ice is older than you think. A 5,000-year-old pair of skates, made from animal bones, has been found in Switzerland. The kind of ice skates we use today first appeared in Holland in the $14^{th}$ century. The Dutch used skates on the frozen canals in winter. They were much faster than walking in the snow. The design of ice skates continued to improve, especially with the use of metal blades. By the $19^{th}$ century people all over the world enjoyed ice skating.

**Roller skates** The idea for roller skates appeared in Holland in the 1700s, in the summertime when there was no more ice. The English, French and Germans tried to make good, safe skates, but it wasn't until 1863 that an American invented skates with four wheels, two at the front and two at the back. They also had a brake at the front, to make it easier to stop. These were the first skates that made it possible to turn left or right.

**Rollerblades** The first time someone put wheels one behind the other on the bottom of shoes was in 1823. The only problem was that skaters couldn't turn left or right – they could only skate in a straight line. 160 years later, an American businessman developed the same idea with different materials, and modern Rollerblades were here. The other characteristic of Rollerblades is that the brake is at the back of the skate, and not at the front.

**3** Match the highlighted words with their meanings.

a a typical part of something *characteristic*
b the part of a roller skate used to stop it ________
c the opposite of *dangerous* ________
d the metal parts underneath ice skates ________
e when something has become ice ________
f wood, metal, glass, or plastic, for example ________

## B Read for general meaning

**4** Match the films and the texts.

**1** This is the second spectacular adventure with Captain Jack Sparrow and his men. This time, Jack has to escape from the horrible Davy Jones, and find the key to the captain's chest. This will solve all his problems, or so he thinks ... It's a fantastic film for all the family, but especially for the kids.

**2** Based on a true story, this is a detective film set in Los Angeles in the 1940s. A young woman is found dead and two policemen investigate the crime. One of them dies, leaving the other to solve the crime himself. The film has some great photography, but in the end is nothing special.

**3** An older man, Justin, and a younger woman, Tessa, meet at a university lecture, and fall in love. He is a quiet man, with a love of gardening, while she is much more outgoing. They get married and move to Kenya, where one day Tessa is killed. Justin decides to investigate the murder, with extremely dangerous results. One moment we get action and the next romance – the result is a thrilling story from start to finish.

**5** Look at the highlighted words in the texts. Try to guess their meanings from the context. When you think you know, check in your dictionary.

## C Listen to identify specific information

6 3S.1▶ Listen to three people talking about a film. Match the speaker with the opinion.

1 ☐ Speaker 1
2 ☐ Speaker 2
3 ☐ Speaker 3

a very good film
b not a bad film
c not interesting

7 Listen again carefully. Match the speakers with the phrases.

a ☐ the photography was great
b ☐ a lot of action
c ☐ it started off really well
d ☐ it looks absolutely amazing
e ☐ it was all right
f ☐ it just got boring

## D Write an answer to an invitation

8 Read the invitation and complete the notes.

*Hi Tony,*

*Are you busy on Friday night? We're going to have a pizza party with some friends from our Italian class. And we're going to watch a video as well – the new Oliver Stone film. I know you love his films! The party starts at 8 o'clock at my house. Why don't you come round?*

*Jenny*

To ____________
From ____________
Activity ____________
Time & place ____________

9 Read Tony's answer to the invitation and complete the notes.

Hi Jenny,

Thanks very much for the invitation. I'd really love to go to the party. The problem is, my cousin's getting married on Friday in Liverpool, and I promised to go to the wedding. Maybe we could watch the film some other time? Have a good time together!

Tony

To ____________
From ____________
Yes or no ____________
If no, reason ____________
Make another suggestion
____________

10 Read the invitation and write your answer. Do not forget to include all the necessary information. Look at Tony's message in exercise 9 to help you.

Hi!
What are you doing at the weekend? Louise and I are going to try skating at the new ice rink in town. Do you want to come with us? We're meeting at the post office at 10.30 on Saturday morning. Send me an email, OK?
Brian

____________
____________
____________
____________
____________
____________
____________
____________
____________
____________

**Now try the Self check on** >> p.78.

# How to ask for things in a hotel

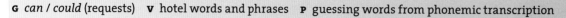

**G** *can / could* (requests) **V** hotel words and phrases **P** guessing words from phonemic transcription

# 4A

## A Vocabulary hotel words and phrases

**1** Find 14 things in a hotel and write them below.

1 *ashtray* ________ 8 ________
2 ________ 9 ________
3 ________ 10 ________
4 ________ 11 ________
5 ________ 12 ________
6 ________ 13 ________
7 ________ 14 ________

**2** Complete the sentences with words from exercise 1.

1 We don't smoke, so we don't need the *ashtray* ________.
2 The ________ doesn't work. Maybe it needs new batteries.
3 I need to wash my hair. Can you get me some ________?
4 There's a problem with the hot water ________. Could you have a look at it, please?
5 My room's not warm enough. I'd like an extra ________, please.
6 I'm sorry, but I get a sore neck if the ________ is too soft. Could you change it for me?
7 I'd love a nice hot bath, but there isn't a clean ________.
8 Would you like a drink from the ________?

## B Grammar *can / could* (requests)

**3** Put the questions in order.

1 shampoo of give another me could bottle you
*Could you give me another bottle of shampoo* ________?
2 call o'clock have I for an alarm could eight
________?
3 me you taxi a order for could
________?
4 towels I some have could clean
________?
5 someone heating the send you check could to
________?

**4** Complete the requests with the best word: *can* or *could*.

1 You want the nurse to bring you some water.
*Could* ________ you bring me some water, please?
2 You want your best friend to close the door.
________ you close the door, please?
3 You want your 60-year-old neighbour to water the plants when you're away on a three-week holiday.
________ you water the plants, please?
4 You need change from an adult near the phone.
________ you give me change, please?
5 You want your wife to pass you the newspaper.
________ you pass the paper, please?

## C Pronunciation guessing words from phonemic transcription

**5** Write the words.

1 /ə'lɑːm kɔːl/ *alarm call*
2 /'aʊtsaɪd laɪn/ ________
3 /kʌp əv 'kɒfi/ ________
4 /'sekənd flɔː/ ________
5 /'dʌbl ruːm/ ________
6 /rɪ'sepʃənɪst/ ________
7 /'kredɪt kɑːd/ ________
8 /ruːm 'sɜːvɪs/ ________

**6** **4A.1▶** Listen and check.

**How well can you ask for things in a hotel now?**
Go back to the Student's Book >> p.37 and tick ✓ the line again.

# How to say what's happened

**G** present perfect for recent events **V** accidents at home **P** short form of *have*

# 4B

## A Vocabulary accidents at home

**1** Complete the phrases with these verbs.

break burn cut drop ~~fall~~ put

1 *fall* off the shelf / out of the fridge / on the floor
2 ________ the toast / your finger / your shirt / your arm / the meat
3 ________ my finger / your hand
4 ________ a window / a plate / a bottle / some glasses
5 ________ an egg / food on the floor / a wet glass
6 ________ salt in the coffee / sugar in the salad / wine in the freezer

## B Grammar present perfect for recent events

**2** Look at the pictures and complete the sentences with a verb from exercise 1. Use the present perfect.

1 He*'s put* the fish in the dishwasher.
2 He ________ the chicken.
3 The plates ________ on the floor.
4 He ________ sugar in the salad.
5 He ________ his finger.
6 He ________ a bottle of wine on the floor.
7 The apples ________ out of the fridge.

**1**

**2**

**6**

**3**

**4**

**5**

**7**

**3** Put the words in order.

1 **A** Your fingers are red!
**B** toaster I've on them the burnt
*I've burnt them on the toaster*!
2 **A** What's wrong?
**B** dropped I've my foot on cup tea of a
________!
3 **A** Are the sandwiches ready?
**B** table yes I've the on put them
________!
4 **A** What was that noise?
**B** Sorry! glass your broken I've
________!
5 **A** Why is John shouting?
**B** bath soap dropped the he's in the
________!
6 **A** Where are the cakes?
**B** Oops! them eaten we've
________!

## C Pronunciation short form of *have*

**4** **4B.1▸** Listen and underline the words you hear.

1 He broke / He's broken a glass.
2 I burnt / I've burnt my trousers.
3 You put / You've put the tea in the coffee pot!
4 She dropped / She's dropped her spoon in the soup!
5 He put / He's put butter in his tea!

**5** Listen again and repeat.

**How well can you say what's happened now?**
Go back to the Student's Book >> p.39 and tick ✓ the line again.

# How to say what you've done

**4C**

G present perfect + - ? V things around the house P when to stress *have*

## A Vocabulary things around the house

**1** Complete the sentences with these words.

gas ~~heating~~ table pillow blanket sofa

1 It's freezing! Can you turn up the *heating* ?
2 If you're cold, I can put another ______ on the bed.
3 Come on everybody! Dinner is on the ______.
4 I can't wait to go to bed and put my head on the ______!
5 It's not cooking, Mum. You have to turn up the ______.
6 Come on. Let's sit on the ______ and watch TV.

**2** Put the words in order to complete the sentences.

1 Wash your face in the *washbasin* (sabashwin).
2 Turn on the ______ (pat) to get water.
3 Use the ______ (spoa) to get clean.
4 To wash your hair, use the ______ (ompasho) in the ______ (orwesh).
5 Use a ______ (ifnek) to cut the food on your ______ (atlep).
6 Use a ______ (frko) to put the food in your mouth.
7 When you have soup, use a ______ (oonsp).
8 ______ (scup) are for tea and coffee; ______ (lsasges) are for milk and juice.
9 When you've finished, put the dirty things in the ______ (snik).

## B Grammar present perfect + - ?

**3** Write what the cleaning lady has done (✓) and what she hasn't done (✗).

1 *She's made the beds*. (make the beds) ✓
2 ______. (do the washing) ✓
3 ______. (put the washing out to dry) ✗
4 ______. (feed the fish) ✗
5 ______. (clean the floor) ✓

**4** Write the questions and answers.

1 *Has she bought the bread*? *No, she hasn't*. (buy the bread) ✗
2 ______? ______. (clean the bathroom) ✓
3 ______? ______. (iron the clothes) ✓
4 ______? ______. (take the dog out) ✗
5 ______? ______. (cook the dinner) ✗

## C Pronunciation when to stress *have*

**5** 4C.1▸ Listen and underline when *have* is stressed.

| | |
|---|---|
| "Have you cleaned your room?<br>Have you brushed your teeth?<br>Have you washed your face?<br>Have you drunk your tea?<br>Have you checked your bag?" | I've cleaned my room<br>I've brushed my teeth<br>But I haven't washed my face<br>And I haven't drunk my tea<br>And I haven't checked my bag<br>– because it's Sunday today! |

**6** Check the audio script on >> p.91.

**7** Listen again and repeat. Copy the stress.

**How well can you say what you've done now?**
Go back to the Student's Book >> p.41 and tick ✓ the line again.

# How to make promises and offers

**G** *will* for promises and offers **V** favours **P** stress in sentences with *will, won't* and *shall*

5B

## A Vocabulary favours

**1** Match the sentences 1–7 with the responses a–g.

1 [e] Wow! Is that the new TV?
2 [ ] It's much colder now than when I arrived!
3 [ ] This is a present for a friend.
4 [ ] Sign these papers here, please.
5 [ ] Here's money for your train fare.
6 [ ] All these bags have to go into the flat.
7 [ ] I've got no money for the taxi!

a Could I borrow your pen?
b No problem! I'll hold the door open for you!
c Thanks – I'll pay you back on Monday.
d Don't worry! We'll pay for it.
e ~~That's right. Can you help me carry it in?~~
f That's fine, sir. We'll wrap it for you.
g Shall I lend you a scarf?

**2** Complete the sentences with these verbs.

borrow carry hold lend ~~pay~~
pay back wear wrap

1 If you buy the food, I'll *pay* ______ for the drinks.
2 Don't forget to ______ your mother's birthday present!
3 I need to open the car. Can you ______ the baby for me?
4 He's going to a wedding, but he doesn't know what to ______.
5 I've left my wallet at home! Can you ______ me £20?
6 If the book is too expensive, you can ______ one from the library.
7 I'll lend you the money if you ______ me ______ by Friday.
8 This box is too heavy! I need someone to help me ______ it upstairs.

## B Grammar *will* for promises and offers

**3** Put the answers in order.

1 **A** You're going away for three weeks!
**B** you I'll day an send every email
*I'll send you an email every day*.

2 **A** Sorry, I have to make an urgent call.
**B** bar wait you we'll the in for
______.

3 **A** I don't feel very well.
**B** of get I'll water you glass a
______.

4 **A** I need to go to Berlin next month.
**B** you room reserve I for a shall
______.

5 **A** I don't want people to know I'm here!
**B** tell I anyone won't
______.

6 **A** I really don't know what to buy!
**B** choose staff help you to our will
______.

7 **A** We arrive at 7.45.
**B** station up you we'll at pick the
______.

8 **A** I just need to look in this shop.
**B** But the bus leaves in twenty minutes!
**A** five be I than minutes more won't
______.

## C Pronunciation stress in sentences with *will, won't* and *shall*

**4** **5B.1▸** Listen and read the sentences.

1 I'll **think about** it.
2 We **won't** be **late**.
3 I'll **see** you **soon**.
4 Shall **I pay** for it?
5 I'll **ask** him **now**.
6 You **won't** be **sorry**.

**5** Listen again and copy the stress. Notice that *won't* is stressed, but *will* and *shall* are not.

**How well can you make promises and offers now?**
Go back to the Student's Book >> p.49 and tick ✓ the line again.

# How to ask for things in shops

**G** phrasal verbs with *on* and *off* **V** shopping phrases **P** sounds spelt with *ea*

5C

## A Vocabulary shopping phrases

**1** Complete the conversations with these phrases.

is fine much better quite big take them do you take ~~I'm looking for~~ try them on how much are they

A [1] *I'm looking for* some new shoes.
B Smart or casual?
A Smart, please.
B What size [2]__________?
A A size 42.
B You'll find them on the left.
A Thank you.

* * *

B Do they fit you, sir?
A Well, they're [3]__________.
B Ah. Here's a smaller size.
A Thanks. I'll [4]__________.
B What do you think, sir?
A Yes, these are [5]__________. [6]__________?
B They're €120.
A Oh! Do you have anything cheaper?
B Well, there's a sale section just behind you.

* * *

B Did you find anything, sir?
A Yes, thank you. This pair [7]__________.
I'll [8]__________, please.

## B Grammar phrasal verbs with *on* and *off*

**2** ~~Cross out~~ the incorrect sentence.

1 Try this blue jacket on. / Try on this blue jacket. / ~~Try on it~~.
2 On your shoes put. / Put them on. / Put on your shoes.
3 Turn the hot water on. / Turn it on. / Turn the hot on water.
4 Take off your boots. / Take off them. / Take your boots off.
5 Turn the engine off. / Turn off it. / Turn off the engine.

**3** Complete the sentences with *on* or *off*. Sometimes there are two possible answers.

1 **A** What's wrong with the tap?
**B** I can't turn it. (off) *I can't turn it off*.
2 I'd like to try this dress, please. (on) __________.
3 **A** It's too hot in here!
**B** I think I'll take my coat. (off) __________.
4 Could you turn the lights, please? (on) __________.
5 **A** You'll need a jacket – it's only 5°C outside!
**B** I'll put it later. (on) __________.

## C Pronunciation sounds spelt with *ea*

**4** Complete the table with the underlined words.

| | |
|---|---|
| Beans please! | nearest and dearest |
| wet weather | What does this mean? |
| My dream team! | apples and pears |
| bread and butter | Great clothes to wear! |
| A late breakfast | A weekend break |

| | |
|---|---|
| /iː/ leave | |
| /eə/ bear | |
| /e/ head | |
| /ɪə/ hear | |
| /eɪ/ steak | |

**5** 5C.1▶ Listen and check.

**6** Listen again and repeat the words.

**7** Add another word to each section of the table.

**How well can you ask for things in shops now?**
Go back to the Student's Book >> p.51 and tick ✓ the line again.

# How to talk about obligations

**6B**

**G** *have to, don't have to, mustn't* **V** on the road **P** *have to*

## A Vocabulary on the road

**1** Complete the crossword.

**Across**

4 pedestrians have to walk on this
6 a wide road where vehicles can travel fast
8 you have to wear this on your head when you ride a motorbike
9 the rubber part of a wheel without enough air in it

**Down**

1 when they are red, you have to stop
2 you have to wear this in a car to keep you safe in an accident
3 a piece of metal on the front and back of your car with numbers and letters on it
5 a person who rides a bicycle
7 you have to put this liquid in your car to make it go

**2** Complete the text with these phrases.

rules of the road   the engine   ~~driving test~~   petrol station   driving licence   traffic police officer   speed limit

Three weeks ago, I passed my 1 *driving test*. The next day, the problems started. First, I couldn't start 2 ________, and had to walk to the nearest 3 ________ for help. I was going to be late for work, so I didn't keep to the 4 ________. Then I heard the sound of a siren behind me – it was a 5 ________. He stopped me and gave me a lecture about the 6 ________. I suppose I was lucky I didn't lose my 7 ________.

## B Grammar *have to, don't have to, mustn't*

**3** Complete the rules for hiring a car with *have to*, *don't have to*, or *mustn't*.

1 You *have to* show your driving licence.
2 You ________ drive without a seat belt.
3 If you get a parking ticket, you ________ pay it yourself. We will not pay it for you.
4 You ________ let anyone else drive the car.
5 You ________ sign the car hire papers. No signature – no car.
6 You ________ pay in cash, but we prefer it if you do.
7 You ________ return the car full of petrol – not almost full, but full.
8 You ________ wash the car, but we'll be very happy if you do.

## C Pronunciation *have to*

**4** **6B.1▸** Listen and tick ✓ the sentence you hear.

1 a ☑ We have to bottle the wine.
  b ☐ We have two bottles of wine.
2 a ☐ We have to colour the drawing.
  b ☐ We have two colour drawings.
3 a ☐ We have to lock the doors.
  b ☐ We have two locks on the doors.
4 a ☐ We have to show tickets.
  b ☐ We have two show tickets.
5 a ☐ We have to fine fast drivers.
  b ☐ We have two fine fast drivers.

**5** Check the audio script on >> p.92.

**6** **6B.2▸** Listen and repeat the phrases. Notice the different pronunciation of *have to* /hæf tə/ and *have two* /hæv tuː/.

| **And you?** Write rules for driving in your country. |
|---|
| *Example You have to drive on the right.* |
| 1 |
| 2 |
| 3 |
| 4 |
| 5 |
| 6 |
| 7 |
| 8 |

**How well can you talk about obligations now?**
Go back to the Student's Book >> p.59 and tick ✓ the line again.

# How to tell a story

6C

**G** past of irregular verbs **V** bank and post office **P** *-ought / -aught* = /ɔːt/

## A Grammar past of irregular verbs

**1** Complete the table with the past simple of these verbs.

~~send~~ ~~open~~ work get have ask look play run call see drive write change find close

| Regular | Irregular |
|---|---|
| *opened* | *sent* |
| | |
| | |
| | |
| | |
| | |
| | |
| | |

**2** Complete the story with the past simple of these verbs.

buy ~~go~~ leave tell take put catch find steal break come

A woman [1] *went* shopping one day and [2] ________ a laptop. She then [3] ________ the laptop in the car and walked to the chemist's, but she [4] ________ her purse in the car. A thief [5] ________ the car window and [6] ________ the car, the purse, the laptop – everything. When the woman [7] ________ back and couldn't find her car, she called the police and [8] ________ them what had happened. The police officers looked around and [9] ________ the purse, but it was empty. So she thanked the police and [10] ________ a taxi home. On the way home, her taxi crashed into a car at the traffic lights – but not just any car, her car! In the end, she [11] ________ the thief herself!

## B Vocabulary bank and post office

**3** Complete the words with *a, e, i, o,* or *u*.

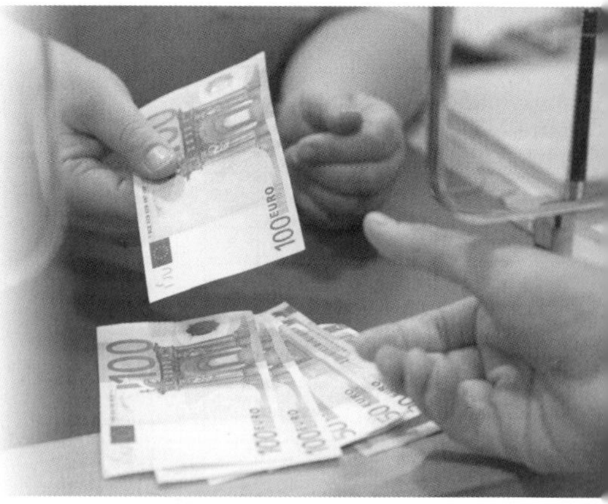

1 What's your <u>a</u>cc<u>ou</u>nt n<u>u</u>mb<u>e</u>r?
2 How would you like the c_sh?
3 Where's the nearest c_sh m_ch_n_, please?
4 Have you got a cr_d_t c_rd?
5 What's your p_st c_d_?
6 The c_sh_ _r is over there on the right.
7 Please write your address on the back of the _nv_l_p_.
8 I'd like to buy tr_v_ll_r's ch_q_ _s for €500, please.

## C Pronunciation *-ought / -aught* = /ɔːt/

**4** Underline the words with the /ɔːt/ sound.

If taught comes from teach
Why doesn't bought come from beach?
And if thought comes from think
Why doesn't brought come from brink?

There's no answer to that, my friend
But you'll learn them all in the end
Bought and brought, taught and thought
For now, just don't get caught!

**5** **6C.1▸** Listen and check.

**6** Listen again and practise saying the rhyme.

**And you?** What did you do last week?

I bought ________________.
I told ________________.
I found ________________.
I wrote ________________.
I lost ________________.
I saw ________________.
I left ________________.
I went ________________.

**How well can you tell a story now?**
Go back to the Student's Book >> p.61 and tick ✓ the line again.

# How to explain what you mean

**G** defining relative clauses **V** jobs, workplaces and tools

7B

## A Vocabulary jobs, workplaces and tools

**1** Who says this? Read the sentences and complete the crossword.

**Across**
2 'Would you like your money in tens or twenties?'
5 'You're in room 213, sir.'
7 'Open wide.'
8 'I'm afraid you need a new engine.'
9 'We'll be coming in to land in about twenty minutes.'

**Down**
1 'Stay still while I put on this bandage.'
3 'This one is oil on canvas.'
4 'I'm sorry but she's in a meeting at the moment.'
6 'Eureka!'

**2** Match the jobs in exercise 1 with the workplaces.

1 bank *cashier*
2 cockpit ______
3 garage ______
4 hospital ______
5 hotel ______
6 laboratory ______
7 office ______
8 studio ______
9 surgery ______

## B Grammar defining relative clauses

**3** Asking for the word when you know the meaning. Complete the questions with *who*, *which*, or *where*.

1 What do you call a person *who* looks after your teeth?
2 What do you call the place ______ people go to borrow books?
3 What do you call the black thing ______ teachers write on?
4 What do you call the place ______ pilots sit?
5 What do you call someone ______ gives you money in a bank?
6 What do you call the thing ______ takes photos?

**4** Answer the questions in exercise 3.

1 *A dentist*.
2 ______.
3 ______.
4 ______.
5 ______.
6 ______.

**5** Asking for the meaning when you know the word. Answer the questions. Use *who*, *which*, or *where*.

1 What's a nurse? *It's a person who works in a hospital*.
2 What's a bank? ______.
3 What's a tractor? ______.
4 What's a mechanic? ______.
5 What's a laboratory? ______.
6 What's a computer? ______.

**And you?** Write definitions for the jobs of your friends and family. Use your dictionary.

*My sister is an optician. An optician is a person who tests people's eyes.*

1

2

3

4

5

How well can you explain what you mean now?
Go back to the Student's Book >> p.69 and tick ✓ the line again.

# How to talk about rules (2)

7C

**G** *can / can't* (permission) **P** short and long *O* /ɒ/ and /əʊ/

## A Grammar *can / can't* (permission)

**1** Complete the rules for visiting a museum with *can* or *can't* and these verbs.

| can | can't |
|---|---|
| ~~ask~~ write press talk | climb drop take touch |

1 You *can ask* questions. ✓
2 You ________ photos. ✗
3 You ________ the buttons on the displays. ✓
4 You ________ on the dinosaurs. ✗
5 You ________ the mummies. ✗
6 You ________ quietly. ✓
7 You ________ notes. ✓
8 You ________ litter. ✗

**2** Put the conversation in order.

A [1] Can I go out with my friends?
A [ ] At about eleven o'clock if I walk.
A [ ] Can I go out when it's finished?
A [ ] No, I haven't.
A [ ] I can't afford a taxi.

B [ ] Then you can't go out.
B [ ] All right! I'll pay for the taxi.
B [2] Have you finished your homework?
B [ ] That depends. What time will you be back?
B [ ] Can't you get a taxi?

**3** Look at these examples of *can* and *can't* from exercise 2. Write *P* for Permission or *A* for Ability.

1 [ ] Can I go out with my friends?
2 [ ] Can I go out when it's finished?
3 [ ] I can't afford a taxi.
4 [ ] Then you can't go out.
5 [ ] Can't you get a taxi?

## B Pronunciation short and long *O* /ɒ/ and /əʊ/

**4** Look at the examples. Write *A* (/ɒ/) or *B* (/əʊ/) next to the phrases.

1 [B] No mobile phones!
2 [ ] Not a lot of coffee.
3 [ ] Tom has gone to the office.
4 [ ] Are you going home alone?
5 [ ] What a lot of chocolate!
6 [ ] No smoking in *my* home!
7 [ ] I hope the hotel's OK.
8 [ ] We've got a lot of hot cakes.

**5** **7C.1▸** Listen and check. Copy the pronunciation.

**And you?** What are the rules in your home / at work / at school? Write four things you *can* do and four things you *can't*.

1
2
3
4
5
6
7
8

**How well can you talk about rules now?**
Go back to the Student's Book >> p.71 and tick ✓ the line again.

# How to describe things

**G** present passive **V** shape and material **P** passive or active?

8B

## A Grammar present passive

**1** Write *A* for active and *P* for passive sentences.

1 ☐ The boats go out early in the morning.
2 ☐ Fishermen catch the fish in the sea.
3 ☐ The fish are taken to the market.
4 ☐ People buy the fish.
5 ☐ The fish are cleaned and cooked.
6 ☐ Families eat the fish for dinner.
7 ☐ The dirty dishes are left for the morning.

**2** Change the active sentences to passive.

1 Someone picks the strawberries.
*The strawberries are picked* ______.

2 A person takes the strawberries to the factory.
______.

3 A machine washes the strawberries.
______.

4 A person cooks the strawberries with sugar and lemon juice.
______.

5 Somebody leaves the jam to cool.
______.

6 Someone sends the jam to the shops.
______.

7 A person sells the jam.
______.

8 People eat the jam on toast for tea.
______.

## B Vocabulary shape and material

**3** Match the objects and the descriptions.

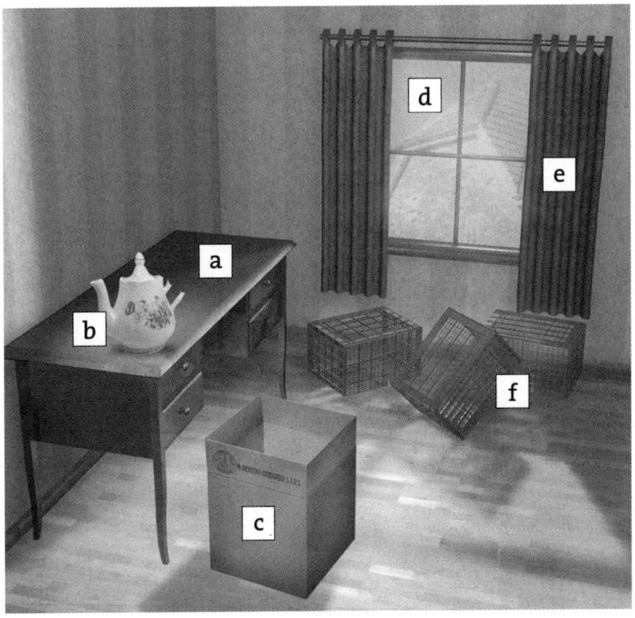


1 ☐ It's big and square, and it's made of cardboard.
2 ☐ It's a big, square thing, made of metal, with four pieces of glass in it.
3 ☐ It's a long, flat thing, made of wood, with four legs.
4 ☐ It's round and made of china, and it's got a broken handle.
5 ☐ They're made of plastic. There are three of them.
6 ☐ They'relong, flat, and made of cloth. There are two of them.

**4** Match the words with the pictures in exercise 3.

1 ☐ cardboard box 4 ☐ desk
2 ☐ plastic crates 5 ☐ teapot
3 ☐ curtains 6 ☐ window

## C Pronunciation passive or active?

**5** **8B.1▸** Listen and <u>underline</u> the words you hear.

1 It / <u>It's</u> painted beautifully.
2 They / They're washed in water.
3 She / She's called Alice.
4 They / They're cooked well.
5 It / It's cleaned badly.
6 I / I'm watched all night.

**6** Check the audio script on >> p.93.

**7** Listen again and copy the pronunciation.

**How well can you describe things now?**
Go back to the Student's Book >> p.79 and tick ✓ the line again.

# How to make predictions

**G** *will* (predictions) **P** *'ll*

8C

## A Grammar *will* (predictions)

**1** Look at the information in the chart. Underline *will* or *won't* to complete the sentences.

| | | THIS YEAR | NEXT YEAR |
|---|---|---|---|
| 1 | price of petrol | €1.10 / litre | €2.00 / litre |
| 2 | minimum salary | €5,000 / year | €5,000 / year |
| 3 | number of schools | 95,000 | 95,000 |
| 4 | number of unemployed people | 4,800,000 | 4,300,000 |
| 5 | number of people over 65 | 14 million | 17 million |
| 6 | number of tourists | 21 million | 22 million |
| 7 | value of things we sell to other countries | €1.5 billion | €1.3 billion |
| 8 | value of things we buy from other countries | €2 billion | €2 billion |

1 The price of petrol will / won't go up.
2 The minimum salary will / won't stay the same.
3 The number of schools will / won't change.
4 There will / won't be fewer unemployed people.

**2** Complete the sentences with *will* or *won't* and the verbs in brackets.

1 There *will be* ________ many more old people (be)
2 More tourists ________ the country. (visit)
3 Our country ________ less to other countries. (sell)
4 We ________ more from other countries. (buy)

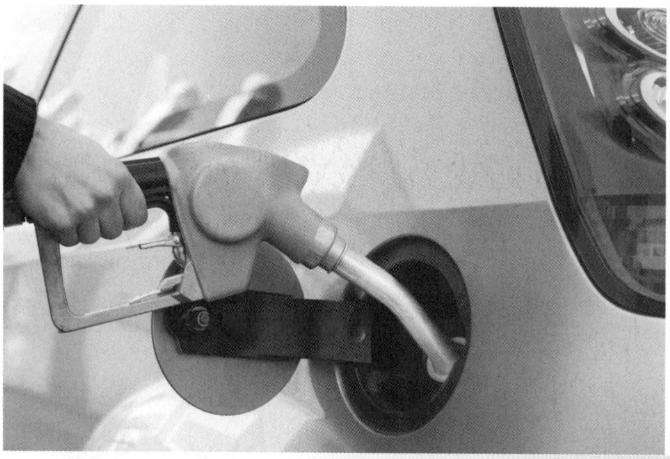

**3** Put the sentences in order.

**She** Are you worried about next year?
**He** Of course I am.
**She** Why?
**He** 1 it'll year a be think difficult I
________________.
**She** Why?
**He** 2 job you'll new in be a because
________________.
**She** And?
**He** 3 exams pass I maybe my won't
________________.
**She** Don't be silly. Of course you'll pass them!
**He** 4 flat be buy we a able to will but
________________?
**She** I'm not sure about that – I hope we can borrow money from the bank.
**He** 5 bank us money won't maybe lend the any
________________!
**She** Oh, don't be such a pessimist!

## B Pronunciation *'ll*

**4** **8C.1▸** Listen and underline the words you hear.

1 I'll / It'll be late!
2 You'll / We'll talk later.
3 He'll / She'll arrive at nine.
4 You'll / They'll ask at the hotel.
5 He'll / We'll tell you the answer!
6 I / I'll write to him.
7 We / We'll catch the train.
8 You / You'll ask the questions.
9 I / I'll take the money.
10 They / They'll send the news.

**5** Check the audio script on >> p.93.

**6** Listen again and repeat.

**How well can you make predictions now?**
Go back to the Student's Book >> p.81 and tick ✓ the line again.

# How to explain how to cook something

**9B**

**G** quantifiers **V** cooking; sequencers

## A Vocabulary cooking; sequencers

**1** Find twelve verbs for cooking in the puzzle.

| | | | | | | | | | |
|---|---|---|---|---|---|---|---|---|---|
| P | T | H | V | I | C | U | T | T | A |
| R | W | E | U | K | B | J | S | P | E |
| C | B | A | R | B | E | C | U | E | M |
| Y | Q | T | R | O | O | H | Z | E | G |
| X | R | T | P | I | H | O | D | L | P |
| G | R | I | L | L | H | P | K | K | O |
| L | O | J | J | T | S | I | W | E | U |
| Z | A | D | U | F | R | Y | A | T | R |
| S | S | T | I | R | C | C | S | A | L |
| Q | T | G | W | J | R | I | H | E | P |

**2** Complete the recipe with these verbs.

boil chop serve fry ~~peel~~ pour stir wash

### Potato omelette

**INGREDIENTS:**

*three eggs*
*two large potatoes*
*oil*
*salt and pepper*

First, 1 *peel* the potatoes and 2 ________ them in cold water. Next, 3 ________ them into small pieces and 4 ________ them in water until they are soft. Then 5 ________ out the water. After that, add the eggs, salt, and pepper to the potatoes and 6 ________. Now, put some oil into a frying pan and 7 ________ everything until cooked. Finally, cut the omelette into six pieces and 8 ________ with mayonnaise or ketchup.

## B Grammar quantifiers

**3** Complete the conversation with these quantifiers.

a few a little a lot none

**Trainee** Shall I put the pepper in now?
**Chef** Yes, but just 1 *a little*! Remember, there isn't much pepper in this recipe!
**T** OK. What about some water? This looks a bit dry.
**C** Yes, we need 2 ________ of water – about 5 litres.
**T** Right! Anything else?
**C** Yes, salt. But only use 3 ________. About twenty grams is fine.
**T** Right!
**C** Oh, and don't forget the potatoes. We only need 4 ________. Use three or four. But wash them first!
**T** Sorry!
**C** And the last thing is the lemon juice. How much juice is there in the fridge?
**T** 5 ________! We used it all yesterday.
**C** Well, go to the shops and buy 6 ________ lemons.
**T** How many?
**C** Three will be fine.

**4** Order the words to make sentences and questions.

1 milk little I a like tea my in
*I like a little milk in my tea*.

2 sugar take how do much you
____________________?

3 potatoes he's for washed few a dinner
____________________.

4 sausages we barbecue lot need of for a the
____________________.

5 this how onions do in many you want
____________________?

6 pour can on a oil my you little salad
____________________?

**How well can you explain how to cook something now?**
Go back to the Student's Book >> p.89 and tick ✓ the line again.

# How to give lifestyle advice

**G** *should* **V** verb phrases with *make, do, have* **P** *should, shouldn't*

9C

## A Grammar *should*

**1** Complete the sentences with *should* or *shouldn't*.

1 You *should* get a haircut.
2 You ______ have a shave.
3 You ______ wash your car.
4 You ______ wear dirty old clothes.
5 You ______ buy some new clothes.
6 You ______ play your radio so loud.
7 You ______ control your children.
8 You ______ move to another town!

## B Vocabulary verb phrases with *make, do, have*

**2** Complete the diary for yesterday with the correct form of *make, do,* or *have*.

*Thursday June 23rd*

*9.30* *I* [1] *had* *a shower.*
*10.00* *I* [2]______ *the bed and* [3]______ *the cleaning.*
*10.30* *I sat down and* [4]______ *a glass of water.*
*11.00* *I* [5]______ *a phone call and went to the gym. In the gym, I* [6]______ *some exercise for an hour.*
*12.30* *I* [7]______ *another shower.*
*13.00* *I* [8]______ *the shopping.*
*16.00* *I* [9]______ *a sleep because I felt tired.*
*17.00* *The cat* [10]______ *a mess, so I had to clean the patio.*
*19.00* *I* [11]______ *my homework because I've got my English class in the morning.*

## C Pronunciation *should, shouldn't*

**3** **9C.1▸** Listen and underline the words you hear.
1 You should / shouldn't go and talk to them.
2 You should / shouldn't get angry.
3 You should / shouldn't spend all your money.
4 You should / shouldn't eat too much.
5 You should / shouldn't think about the future.
6 You should / shouldn't worry about the past.

**4** Check the audio script on >> p.93.

**5** In which sentence do you hear the *t* in *shouldn't* /ʃʊdn(t)/?

**6** Listen again and practise saying the sentences.

| **And you?** Give advice for your family. |
|---|
| My father ... |
| My mother ... |
| My brother / sister ... |
| My cousin ... |
| My aunt ... |
| My uncle ... |
| My husband / wife ... |
| My son / daughter ... |

**How well can you give lifestyle advice now?**
Go back to the Student's Book >> p.91 and tick ✓ the line again.

# How to talk about table manners



**G** *should* and *must*

## A Grammar *should* and *must*

**1** ~~Cross out~~ the verb which is NOT correct.

1 You should / ~~shouldn't~~ / must say 'please' when you ask for something.
2 Visitors in a hospital must / shouldn't / mustn't make a lot of noise.
3 You mustn't / shouldn't / must smoke on the train.
4 It's raining now, so you must / mustn't / should take an umbrella.
5 If you want to lose weight, you shouldn't / should / mustn't eat so much chocolate.
6 People mustn't / must / should control their dogs in the street.

**2** Match the sentences and their meanings.

1 ☐ You should use your hands to break bread.
2 ☐ You shouldn't cut your bread with a knife.
3 ☐ You must eat with your fingers if the locals do.
4 ☐ You mustn't touch the food with your left hand.

a Do this. It's very bad manners not to.
b It's polite to do this.
c Don't do this. It's very bad manners.
d It isn't polite to do this.

**3** Write sentences with *must*, *mustn't*, *should*, or *shouldn't*.

1 speak with your mouth full (it isn't polite)
*You shouldn't speak with your mouth full* .
2 eat at the table (it's very bad manners not to)
____________ .
3 talk quietly during a meal (it's polite)
____________ .
4 drink from a soup bowl (it isn't polite)
____________ .
5 put your elbows on the table (it isn't polite)
____________ .
6 wait until everyone has finished before leaving the table (it's very bad manners not to)
____________ .
7 finish all the food on your plate (it's polite)
____________ .
8 put the knife in your mouth (it's very bad manners)
____________ .
9 say 'thank you' to the cook (it's polite)
____________ .

**And you?** Complete the sentences. In my family, ...

you can ____________ .
you should ____________ .
you shouldn't ____________ .
you must ____________ .
you mustn't ____________ .
you have to ____________ .
you don't have to ____________ .

**How well can you talk about table manners now?**
Go back to the Student's Book >> p.93 and tick ✓ the line again.

# Unit 9 Skills Practice

## A Read and understand a recipe

**1** Read the ingredients for the Spanish dish 'gazpacho'. It is a cold soup made from vegetables. Are any of the words the same in your language?

**Gazpacho** – 1 clove of garlic
50 grams dry bread
100 ml olive oil
500 grams fresh tomatoes
500 ml water
some salt and vinegar

**2** Read the instructions and put the pictures in order.

1 First of all, put the tomatoes in the blender and make juice.
2 Next, add the dry bread. Leave for ten minutes.
3 Then, add the garlic, oil, salt, and vinegar.
4 After that, blend everything together.
5 Check the taste. Add more salt and vinegar if necessary.
6 Now add the water.
7 Finally, serve cold with ice cubes.

## B Read restaurant reviews

**3** Read the reviews quickly and write *true* or *false*.

1 The Parkers drink a lot of beer. ________
2 Helen Turner went to the restaurant with her family. ________
3 Smith and Wilson are smokers. ________

**A**

We visited The Lake Café on a Friday evening. A friend of mine recommended it. We thought the atmosphere was nice – comfortable, quiet, the kind of place where you can enjoy your conversation. The food was good, but the service was very slow. We had to send the main course back because it was cold. The selection of wines was also a bit limited – we expected a bigger choice. Parking is definitely a problem. There's only space for ten cars outside, and it's in a busy street near the town centre. The prices are reasonable, but we thought the desserts were a bit small.

JOHN & ISABEL PARKER

**B**

We had lunch at The Lake Café last Saturday. It was very busy, and we were lucky to get a table. We liked the food a lot. There's a good choice on the menu (and my husband's a vegetarian) and the portions are generous. We also liked the beers. They serve a lot of local beers, and they serve them cold, which is great in the hot summer weather. The service wasn't too bad. They brought the children's meals first, but ours took a bit longer. I didn't like the quality of the children's meals very much. It looked like frozen food from the supermarket. The other thing I didn't like much was the atmosphere. It's a bit dark, and too quiet for a restaurant. I think they should have music or TV to make the place more natural. But I must say the prices are great.

HELEN TURNER

**C**

We stopped at The Lake Café for dinner on Thursday after some late shopping, but we wouldn't recommend it, really. I didn't like the food at all. The portions were all right, but it just didn't taste very good. We asked for a non-smokers' table and they put us next to the smoking area, so that didn't help. The atmosphere was good, though. No loud music or TV, so you can hear each other properly. Oh yes, and I think they could clean the toilets more often. Also the prices are too high for the kind of food they serve. We wouldn't give this place any Michelin stars!

BRIAN SMITH & TOM WILSON

4 Read the reviews again more carefully and answer the questions.

1 Who enjoyed the atmosphere? *A* and ____
2 Who thought the desserts should be bigger? ____
3 Who wasn't happy about the prices? ____
4 Who didn't like the lighting? ____
5 Who doesn't say anything about the drinks? ____
6 Who didn't like the service? ____
7 Who was unhappy with the children's food? ____
8 Who thought there should be better parking facilities? ____
9 Which review is the most negative? ____

5 Choose five words from the text to check in your dictionary. Write the meaning and pronunciation in your vocabulary notebook.

## C Listen for personal preferences

6 9S.1▶ Listen to three people talking about the kind of food they prefer. Match the speakers with the pictures.

a ☐

b ☐

c ☐

7 Listen again and complete the table with these phrases.

fruit and a yogurt two-course meal three-course meal glass of hot milk a light breakfast ~~toast or cereals~~ Italian, Turkish sausage and egg rice or pasta

| | Janet | Henry | Olga |
|---|---|---|---|
| **breakfast** | 1 *toast or cereals* | 4 | 7 |
| **lunch** | 2 | 5 | 8 |
| **supper** | 3 | 6 | 9 |

## D Write about your favourite dish

8 Complete the text with *also, and,* or *as well.*

One of my favourite dishes is Russian salad. My grandmother always made it for me when I was a child. You can change some of the ingredients, but we normally use potatoes, peas, tuna fish, a hard-boiled egg, sweetcorn 1________ grated carrot. You 2________ need mayonnaise for the sauce.

First, cut the potatoes into cubes, boil them 3________ leave them to cool. Cut the egg into small pieces. Mix everything together in a bowl, then add the mayonnaise 4________. Serve the salad cold, decorated with pieces of baked red pepper. If you like, you can 5________ use black olives.

9 Make notes for your favourite dish.

| | |
|---|---|
| Name of dish | |
| Why I like it | |
| Ingredients | |
| How to make it | |

10 Now write about your favourite dish.

____________________
____________________
____________________
____________________
____________________
____________________
____________________

Now try the Self check on >> p.84.

# How to say where places are

**v** places; journey times

# 10A

## A Vocabulary places; journey times

**1** Complete the sentences about Sri Lanka with *in* or *on*.

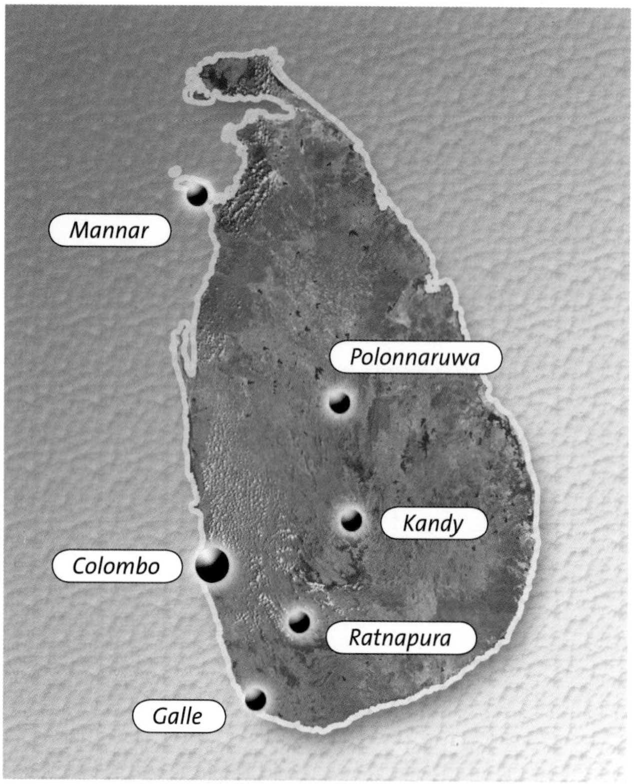


1 Sri Lanka is an island *in* the Indian Ocean.
2 Colombo, the capital, is ________ the west coast.
3 Kandy, the old capital, is ________ a lake ________ the centre of the island.
4 Galle is a well-known beach town ________ the south.
5 You can see the famous rock Buddhas ________ the centre, near Polonnaruwa.
6 Why not visit the rock palace of Sigiriya ________ the northern forests?
7 If the weather ________ the coast is too hot, you could stay ________ the town of Nuwara Eliya ________ the mountains.
8 You can buy lots of gems ________ Ratnapura, a town ________ the river Kalu Ganga.
9 Anuradhapura, ________ the north-central district, is a UNESCO site.
10 If you want to cross to India, you can take the ferry ________ Mannar Island.

**2** Look at the pictures and complete the phrases.

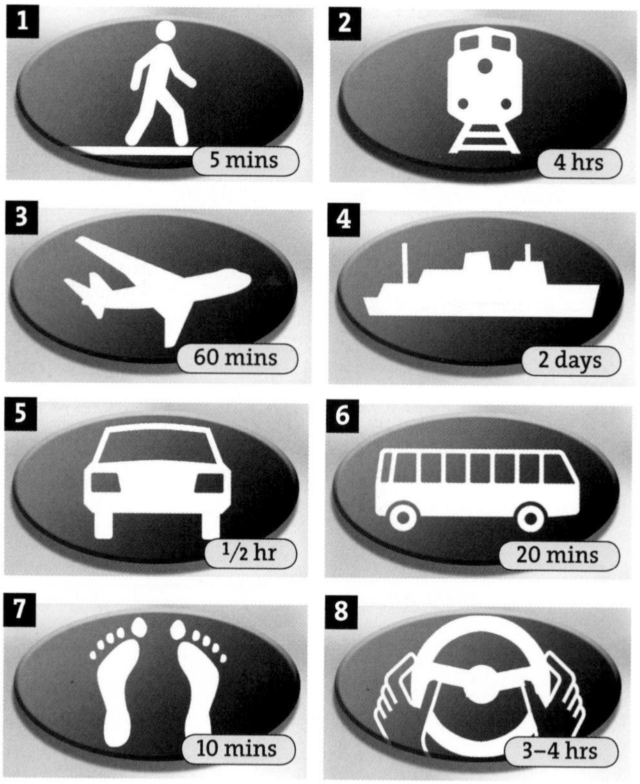


1 a f*ive* -m*inute* w*alk*
2 f________ h________ b________ tr________
3 a s________ -m________ fl________
4 a t________ -d________ b________ j________
5 a h________ -h________ dr________
6 a t________ -m________ b________ r________
7 t________ m________ o________ f________
8 th________ o________ f________ h________ b________ c________

**3** Match the cities with their pronunciation.

| | | | |
|---|---|---|---|
| 1 | [c] Bordeaux | a | /ˈedɪnbrə/ |
| 2 | [ ] Cologne | b | /ˈvenɪs/ |
| 3 | [ ] Edinburgh | c | ~~/bɔːˈdəʊ/~~ |
| 4 | [ ] Geneva | d | /dʒəˈniːvə/ |
| 5 | [ ] Lisbon | e | /kəˈləʊn/ |
| 6 | [ ] Venice | f | /ˈlɪsbən/ |
| 7 | [ ] Vienna | g | /ˈwɔːsɔː/ |
| 8 | [ ] Warsaw | h | /viːˈenə/ |

**4** **10A.1▸** Listen and check.

**How well can you say where places are now?**
Go back to the Student's Book >> p.97 and tick ✓ the line again.

# How to talk about stages of a journey **10B**

**G** present perfect with *yet*, *just* and *already* **V** air travel **P** *yet* /j/ or *jet* /dʒ/

## A Vocabulary air travel

**1** Put the letters in order to complete the phrases.

1 *arrive* at the airport. (~~evirra~~)
2 ________ your bags. (hekcc ni)
3 go through ________ control (stoppars)
4 visit the ________ shop (ytud efer)
5 go to the ________ gate (perturdae)
6 ________ the plane (dobar)
7 relax while the plane ________ (steak fof)
8 look out of the window as the plane ________ (snald)
9 ________ your bags (clectol)
10 go through ________ (stumcos)

**2** Complete the text with some of the phrases from exercise 1.

Don't talk to me about airport security! I mean, we travelled back on the tenth, you know, when it all happened. When our taxi [1] *arrived* at the airport, there were police everywhere. It took us more than two hours to [2] ________ the bags. And they asked so many questions at [3] ________ control! We didn't have time to stop at the [4] ________ shop, and we had to run to the [5] ________ gate. But that was a false alarm. They made us wait 90 minutes before we could [6] ________ the plane. When the plane finally [7] ________, we were three hours late! 'We hope you enjoyed your flight today!' they said. They were joking! I couldn't **begin** to relax until we went through [8] ________ and took a taxi into town.

## B Grammar present perfect with *yet*, *just* and *already*

**3** Match the questions 1–8 and answers a–h.

1 [*f*] Have you written to your mother recently?
2 [ ] What's your new book like?
3 [ ] Have you finished your homework yet?
4 [ ] When are you going to buy some new clothes?
5 [ ] Have you passed your driving test yet?
6 [ ] Is your father at home?
7 [ ] Have you called your grandmother yet?
8 [ ] You look a bit tired today!

a Yes, they've already sent me my driving licence.
b Yes, I've spoken to her already.
c I don't know. I haven't read it yet.
d I haven't got enough money yet.
e Yes, I know. I've just woken up!
f ~~I've just sent her a letter.~~
g No, he's just gone out.
h I've already done two exercises.

**4** Write present perfect sentences and questions.

1 you / have lunch / yet
*Have you had lunch yet* ?
2 I / just / speak / Jon
________.
3 Peter / not / call / yet
________.
4 I / already / make / bed
________.
5 Sheila / just / make / tea
________.
6 You / already / break / two plates today
________!
7 just / start / rain
________.
8 you / tidy / room / yet
________?

## C Pronunciation *yet* /j/ or *jet* /dʒ/

**5** **10B.1▸** Listen and underline where you hear the sounds /j/ or /dʒ/.

1 <u>Y</u>ou told me the <u>y</u>oung man died six <u>y</u>ears later!
2 George has got a job as a journalist.
3 Join our cruise in June, July, or August!
4 Have you tried that yellow fruit yet?
5 Have they seen *Bridget Jones' Diary*?
6 Scotland Yard say they found the yacht yesterday.

**6** Check the audio script on >> p.93.

**7** Listen again and repeat.

**How well can you talk about stages of a journey now?**
Go back to the Student's Book >> p.99 and tick ✓ the line again.

# How to keep a conversation going

# 10C

**G** present perfect with *for* and *since* **P** *How long have you ...* questions and answers

## A Grammar present perfect with *for* and *since*

**1** Complete the sentences about Sonia with *for* or *since*.

1 She's lived in London *since* 1985.
2 She's known her best friend ______ she was 19.
3 She's had the same car ______ 18 years.
4 She's had her flat ______ 1998.
5 She's had her dog ______ about seven years.
6 She's been a mother ______ five years.

| | |
|---|---|
| 1970 | born in Liverpool |
| 1985 | moved to London |
| 1988 | got a job in an office |
| 1989 | met her best friend |
| 1990 | bought a car |
| 1995 | met her boyfriend |
| 1998 | bought a flat |
| 2000 | got married |
| 2001 | got a dog and a cat |
| 2003 | had a baby |
| 2005 | became a vegetarian |
| 2007 | joined a sports club |
| 2008 | TODAY |

**2** Complete the sentences about Sonia. Use the present perfect and these verbs.

~~work~~ have know be (×2) not eat

1 She *'s worked* in an office since 1988.
2 She ______ her husband for thirteen years.
3 She ______ married since she was 30.
4 She ______ a cat since 2001.
5 She ______ meat since 2005.
6 She ______ a member of a sports club for a year.

## B Pronunciation *How long have you ...* questions and answers

**3** Match the questions 1–6 and answers a–f.

1 [c] How long have you had your watch?
2 [ ] How long have you known your friend?
3 [ ] How long have you been at school?
4 [ ] How long have you lived in town?
5 [ ] How long have you played a sport?
6 [ ] How long have you kept a diary?

a Since 1996. We moved here from the country.
b For a long time. But don't ask – you can't read it!
c ~~Since Christmas. My wife gave it to me.~~
d For two years. But I'm not very good.
e Since I was five. But I'm leaving next year.
f For years. We met at school.

**4** **10C.1▶** Listen and check.

**5** Listen again and repeat. Copy the intonation of the questions.

**And you?** Answer the questions.

1 Are you a student?
How long have you been a student?

2 Do you have any pets?
How long have you had them?

3 Who are your best friends?
How long have you known them?

4 Are you married?
How long have you been married?

5 Where do you live?
How long have you lived there?

6 Have you got a driving licence?
How long have you had it?

**How well can you keep a conversation going now?**
Go back to the Student's Book >> p.101 and tick ✓ the line again.

English Result Pre-intermediate Workbook Answer Key Booklet

McKenna

OXFORD

OXFORD
UNIVERSITY PRESS

www.oup.com/elt



CEF
B1
A2
A1

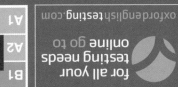

OXFORD ENGLISH
ISBN 978-0-19-430491-7

OXFORD
UNIVERSITY PRESS
Great Clarendon Street, Oxford OX2 6DP

Oxford University Press is a department of the University of Oxford. It furthers the University's objective of excellence in research, scholarship, and education by publishing worldwide in

Oxford New York

Auckland Cape Town Dar es Salaam Hong Kong Karachi Kuala Lumpur Madrid Melbourne Mexico City Nairobi New Delhi Shanghai Taipei Toronto

With offices in

Argentina Austria Brazil Chile Czech Republic France Greece Guatemala Hungary Italy Japan Poland Portugal Singapore South Korea Switzerland Thailand Turkey Ukraine Vietnam



First published 2008
2012 2011 2010 2009 2008
10 9 8 7 6 5 4 3 2 1



ISBN: 978 0 19 430491 7

Printed and bound by Eigal S. A. in Portugal

# Unit 12

12

## 12A

**1**
1 to arrive
2 waiting
3 to come
4 listening
5 to go
6 to play
7 to send
8 calling

**2**
1 standing
2 buying
3 having to
4 to eat
5 to travel; to be
6 watching
7 to sit; to catch

**3**
1 Would you like to come this way?
2 Would you mind giving me your phone number?
3 Could you help me with my bags?
4 Would you like to sign your name?
5 Would you mind calling back in five minutes?
6 Could you call a taxi for me?

**4**
a 3
b 2
c 5
d 1
e 4
f 6

## 12B

**1**
1 d
2 f
3 h
4 a
5 g
6 e
7 c
8 b

**2**
1 anyone
2 anywhere
3 someone
4 No one
5 everyone
6 everyone
7 something
8 somewhere
9 nowhere
10 anything

**3**
1 a ceremony
2 traditional costumes
3 a competition
4 a colourful celebration

**4**
1 station
2 imagination
3 presentation
4 location
5 invitation

## 12C

**1**
1 I'll have
2 are you doing
3 I'll carry
4 we're going
5 I'm flying
6 you'll
7 I'll come
8 I'm going to decide

**2**
1 **A** Are you busy this weekend?
2 **B** Yes, I am, actually. I'm going rock climbing.
3 **A** Have you done it before?
4 **B** No, but I think it'll be fun.
5 **A** Fun? Isn't it a bit dangerous?
6 **B** Oh, stop worrying. I promise I'll be careful.
7 **A** Will you phone me when you get to the top?
8 **B** I'm not going to take my phone! It could get broken!

**3**
1 anything
2 fancy
3 about
4 Would
5 busy

a rather
b Nothing
c prefer
d Maybe
e Let

**4**
1 b
2 e
3 a
4 d
5 c

**5**
1 but I'm afraid I can't.
2 I'll see you tonight.
3 but I've already got plans. Sorry.
4 What time shall we meet?
5 but I haven't got time. Sorry!

## 12D

**1**
1 e
2 c
3 f
4 a
5 g
6 b
7 d
8 h

**2**
1 recycled, would save
2 made, would live
3 put, would be
4 ate, would be
5 turned off, would use
6 used, would get

**3**
1 If I could, I would visit every country in the world.
2 If I were rich, I would buy you a new car.
3 If I had a time machine, I would go to the future.
4 If she asked me to marry her, I would say 'yes'.
5 If I were an animal, I would be a blue whale.
6 If he really loved me, he would tell me.

## Skills Practice

**1**
1 What **is** the Edinburgh Festival?
2 What happens at the Festival?
3 When is it on?
4 How do I get there?
5 Where can I stay?
6 Where can I get tickets?

**2**
1 False
2 True
3 False
4 False
5 True
6 False
7 False
8 False

**3**
1 set up
2 performances
3 fireworks
4 hourly

**5**
1 visit art galley
2 see a film
3 orchestra
4 dinner
5 dance show

**6**
1 Fri.
2 Sat.
3 Aug.
4 St.
5 No.
6 incl.

**7** a

**8**
1 Sasha
2 Linda
3 Marco
4 Marco
5 Rudiger
6 Rudiger

**10**
1 Hi, how are you?
2 you're OK
3 Anyway
4 It's like
5 and things like that
6 You'd love it here
7 See you

# Unit 11

## 11A

**1**
1 doctor's
2 symptoms
3 cough
4 stomach ache
5 sore throat
6 backache
7 headache
8 temperature
9 aspirin

**2**
1 c
2 d
3 f
4 b
5 a
6 e

**3**
1 How do you feel?
2 What's the matter?
3 Have you taken anything for it?
4 Get well soon!
5 You look a lot better.

**4**
1 What's the matter?
2 Have you taken anything for it?
3 How do you feel?
4 You look a lot better.
5 Get well soon!

## 11B

**1**
1 is standing
2 is writing
3 don't know
4 seems
5 is looking
6 think
7 is moving
8 wants
9 is watching
10 Do you remember

**2**
1 's sitting
2 think
3 don't remember
4 seems
5 's looking
6 don't want
7 's preparing
8 wants
9 's waiting

## 11C

**1**
1 decided
2 tried
3 prefer
4 promised
5 refused
6 agreed
7 pretended
8 forgot
9 wanted

**2**
1 She forgot to take her umbrella.
2 He promised to visit me at the weekend.
3 He wants to go home early today.
4 She decided to move to Paris.
5 He prefers to arrive at six o'clock.

**3** *Example answers*
1 She refused to take his money.
2 We agreed to meet at the station.
3 They're planning to fly in April.
4 She's hoping to pass the exam.
5 He tried to open the door.

**4**
1 reason
2 suggest
3 decide
4 finger
5 prefer
6 compare
7 answer

## 11D

**1** **Across**
2 eyebrows
5 ears
6 skin
9 eyelashes
10 cheeks

**Down**
1 forehead
3 lips
4 nose
7 neck
8 chin

**2**
1 was built
2 was completed
3 was not designed
4 worked
5 was done
6 were hired
7 were brought
8 were transported

**3**
1 was used
2 was taken
3 was put
4 was kept
5 was stolen
6 wasn't found
7 weren't arrested
8 were never discovered
9 was repaired
10 was returned

## Skills Practice

**1** d

**2** **Do** b, c, d, f, h, k
**Don't** a, e, g, i, j, l

**3**
1 on your own
2 locked away
3 by mistake
4 out of reach
5 out-of-date

**4**
1 b
2 c
3 d
4 e
5 a

**5**
1 do me a favour
2 queries
3 proper
4 notify

**7**
a 2
b 1
c 4
d 3

**8**
1 four
2 three
3 hundreds
4 four

**10**
1 date and time
2 place
3 cars
4 drivers
5 accident
6 Clearly
7 Finally

# Unit 10

10

## 10A

**1**
1 in
2 on
3 on, in
4 in
5 in
6 in
7 on, in, in
8 in, on
9 in
10 on

**2**
1 a five-minute walk
2 four hours by train
3 a sixty-minute flight
4 a two-day boat journey
5 a half-hour drive
6 a twenty-minute bus ride
7 ten minutes on foot
8 three or four hours by car

**3**
1 c
2 e
3 a
4 d
5 f
6 b
7 h
8 g

**5**
1 You told me the young man died six years later!
2 George has got a job as a journalist.
3 Join our cruise in June, July or August!
4 Have you tried that yellow fruit yet?
5 Have they seen *'Bridget Jones' Diary'*?
6 Scotland Yard say they found the yacht yesterday.

**6**
1 a
2 a
3 b
4 b
5 a
6 b

## 10B

**1**
1 arrive
2 check in
3 passport
4 duty free
5 departure
6 board
7 takes off
8 lands
9 collect
10 customs

**2**
1 arrived
2 check in
3 passport
4 duty free
5 departure
6 board
7 landed
8 customs

**3**
1 f
2 c
3 h
4 d
5 a
6 g
7 b
8 e

**4** *Example answers*
1 Have you had lunch yet?
2 I've just spoken to Jon.
3 Peter hasn't called yet.
4 I've already made the bed.
5 Sheila has just made tea.
6 You've already broken two plates today!
7 It's just started to rain.
8 Have you tidied your room yet?

## 10C

**1**
1 since
2 since
3 for
4 since
5 for
6 for

**2**
1 's worked
2 's known
3 's been
4 's had
5 hasn't eaten
6 's been

**3**
1 c
2 f
3 e
4 a
5 d
6 b

## 10D

**1**
a 3
b 2
c 1

**2**
1 along
2 until
3 reach
4 end
5 takes

**3**
1 used to walk
2 used to be
3 used to send
4 used to travel
5 used to go
6 used to stay

**4**
1 I used to live in America when I was a child.
2 My dad used to wear a tie in his last job.
3 As a teenager, I used to go to a lot of parties.
4 I used to shop at the old market before they built the supermarket.
5 We used to buy CDs every weekend in our teenage years.
6 I used to sleep until ten o'clock every morning at university.

## Skills Practice

**1**
1 Kyoto
2 Tokyo
3 500 kms
4 twelve days
5 twenty hours
6 two and a half hours

**2**
1 d
2 b
3 e
4 c
5 a

**3** Cheapest Isn't Always Best

**4**
1 India
2 Beirut
3 Prague
4 Amsterdam

**5**
1 False
2 True
3 False
4 True

**6**
1 Apartheid Museum
2 Soweto
3 Muldersdrift
4 Gold Reef City
5 Pilanesberg

**7**
a Apartheid Museum
b Pilanesberg
c Gold Reef City
d Soweto
e Muldersdrift

**8**
a 4
b 3
c 5
d 1
e 2

**9**
1 We've already seen
2 We've also
3 we didn't visit it
4 We've just come back
5 We haven't been there yet

**10**
1 Edinburgh
2 windy, but it hasn't rained very much
3 the Castle, the Royal Mile
4 the views, the shops
5 it's windy, the Castle is expensive
6 have a picnic in the Botanical Gardens

# Unit 9

## 9A

**1** **Countable**: a boiled egg, fried eggs, a baked potato, some boiled peas
**Uncountable**: some scrambled egg, some sliced bread, some grated cheese, some grilled fish, some mashed potato

**2**
1 a cup of black coffee
2 a plate of grilled fish
3 four spoons of olive oil
4 a glass of cold water/a cold glass of water
5 500 grams of brown rice
6 two slices of wholemeal bread

**3**
1 a
2 c
3 b
4 f
5 h
6 e
7 d
8 i
9 g

**4**
1 scrambled
2 boiled
3 scrambled
4 boiled
5 sliced
6 mashed
7 roasted

**5**
1 some grated apple
2 some fresh oranges
3 some fried onions
4 some boiled eggs
5 some olive oil

## 9B

**1** barbecue, boil, chop, cut, fry, grill, heat, peel, pour, roast, stir, wash

**2**
1 peel
2 wash
3 chop
4 boil
5 pour
6 stir
7 fry
8 serve

**3**
1 a little
2 a lot
3 a little
4 a few
5 None
6 a few

**4**
1 I like a little milk in my tea.
2 How much sugar do you take?
3 He's washed a few potatoes for dinner.
4 We need a lot of sausages for the barbecue.
5 How many onions do you want in this?
6 Can you pour a little oil on my salad?

## 9C

**1**
1 should
2 should
3 should
4 shouldn't
5 should
6 shouldn't
7 should
8 should

**2**
1 had
2 made
3 did
4 had
5 made
6 did
7 had
8 did
9 had
10 made
11 did

**3**
1 should
2 shouldn't
3 shouldn't
4 shouldn't
5 should
6 shouldn't

**5** You shouldn't eat too much.

## 9D

**1**
1 shouldn't
2 must
3 must
4 mustn't
5 should
6 mustn't

**2**
1 b
2 d
3 a
4 c

**3** *Example answers*
1 You shouldn't speak with your mouth full.
2 You must eat at the table.
3 You should talk quietly during a meal.
4 You shouldn't drink from a soup bowl.
5 You shouldn't put your elbows on the table.
6 You must wait until everyone has finished before leaving the table.
7 You should finish all the food on your plate.
8 You mustn't put the knife in your mouth.
9 You should say 'thank you' to the cook.

## Skills Practice

**2**
a 4
b 6
c 1
d 3
e 7
f 2
g 5

**3**
1 False
2 True
3 False

**4**
1 a, c
2 a
3 c
4 b
5 c
6 a
7 b
8 a
9 c

**6**
1 b
2 c
3 a

**7**
1 toast or cereals
2 two-course meal
3 glass of hot milk
4 sausage and egg
5 three-course meal
6 Italian, Turkish
7 a light breakfast
8 rice or pasta
9 fruit and a yogurt

**8**
1 and
2 also
3 and
4 as well
5 also

# Unit 8

8

## 8A

**1**
1 Their camera is much better than ours!
2 His CD player doesn't work, so he borrowed mine.
3 My laptop's a lot faster than yours!
4 When my TV doesn't work, I watch theirs.
5 She's using his car because hers is in the garage.
6 Your computer games aren't as good as his.

**2**
1 his
2 mine
3 yours
4 mine
5 yours
6 his
7 mine

**3**
1 c, e
2 f
3 b
4 a
5 d

**4**
1 **A** Er, John, is this your CD?
2 **B** Yes it is! Did you like it?
3 **A** Yes, it was great. But I think I've broken it.
4 **B** Oh no! What happened?
5 **A** My brother stood on it by accident. I'm really sorry.
6 **B** That was a present from Cathy.
7 **A** Look, I'll get you another one, OK?
8 **B** Yeah, OK. No problem.
9 **A** Thanks.

**5**
1 me
2 sorry
3 worry
4 so
5 OK
6 mind
7 sure
8 Thanks

## 8B

**1**
1 A
2 A
3 P
4 A
5 P
6 A
7 P

**2**
1 The strawberries are picked.
2 The strawberries are taken to the factory.
3 The strawberries are washed.
4 The strawberries are cooked with sugar and lemon juice.
5 The jam is left to cool.
6 The jam is sent to the shops.
7 The jam is sold.
8 The jam is eaten on toast for tea.

**3**
1 c
2 d
3 a
4 b
5 f
6 e

**4**
1 c
2 f
3 e
4 a
5 b
6 d

**5**
1 It's
2 They
3 She
4 They're
5 It's
6 I

## 8C

**1**
1 will
2 will
3 won't
4 will

**2**
1 will be
2 will visit
3 will sell
4 won't buy

**3**
1 I think it'll be a difficult year.
2 Because you'll be in a new job.
3 Maybe I won't pass my exams.
4 But will we be able to buy a flat?
5 Maybe the bank won't lend us any money!

**4**
1 It'll
2 We'll
3 He'll
4 They'll
5 He'll
6 I
7 We'll
8 You
9 I'll
10 They'll

## 8D

**1**
1 message
2 click on
3 window
4 attachment
5 button
6 window
7 delete

**2**
1 b
2 c
3 a
4 f
5 e
6 d

**3**
1 drive
2 drive
3 will take
4 won't be
5 will save
6 will have to go

## Skills Practice

**2**
1 A
2 P
3 C
4 C
5 A
6 C
7 P
8 P
9 A
10 P

**4**
1 life
2 fate
3 heart
4 head
5 marriage

**5**
1 healthy
2 doesn't really know what they want in life
3 unemotional
4 remembers

**7**
1 False
2 True
3 True
4 False

**8**
2 bat

**9**
1 and
2 because
3 also
4 because
5 and
6 because

# Unit 7

7

## 7A

**1**
1 c
2 f
3 a
4 g
5 d
6 b
7 h
8 e

**2**
1 two-year contract
2 travel expenses
3 competitive salary
4 uniform provided
5 clean driving licence
6 flexible working hours

**3**
1 appearance
2 contract
3 staff
4 qualified
5 experience
6 flexible
7 uniform
8 licence

**4**
1 S
2 S
3 R
4 S
5 R
6 S

## 7B

**1** **Across**
2 cashier
5 receptionist
7 dentist
8 mechanic
9 pilot

**Down**
1 nurse
3 artist
4 secretary
6 scientist

**2**
1 cashier
2 pilot
3 mechanic
4 nurse
5 receptionist
6 scientist
7 secretary
8 artist
9 dentist

**3**
1 who
2 where
3 which
4 where
5 who
6 which

**4**
1 A dentist.
2 A library.
3 A blackboard.
4 A cockpit.
5 A cashier.
6 A camera.

**5** *Example answers*
1 It's a person who works in a hospital.
2 It's a place where a cashier works.
3 It's a thing which farmers use.
4 It's a person who fixes cars.
5 It's a place where scientists work.
6 It's a thing which people use at work.

## 7C

**1**
1 can ask
2 can't take
3 can press
4 can't climb
5 can't touch
6 can talk
7 can write
8 can't drop

**2**
1 **A** Can I go out with my friends?
2 **B** Have you finished your homework?
3 **A** No, I haven't.
4 **B** Then you can't go out.
5 **A** Can I go out when it's finished?
6 **B** That depends. What time will you be back?
7 **A** At about eleven o'clock if I walk.
8 **B** Can't you get a taxi?
9 **A** I can't afford a taxi.
10 **B** All right! I'll pay for the taxi.

**3**
1 P
2 P
3 A
4 P
5 A

**4**
1 B
2 A
3 A
4 B
5 A
6 B
7 B
8 A

## 7D

**1**
1 because
2 so
3 because
4 so
5 because
6 because
7 so
8 because

**2**
1 c
2 a
3 e
4 f
5 b
6 d

**3**
1 a
2 b
3 a
4 b
5 a
6 b

## Skills Practice

**1**
1 He's Luiz Inácio Lula da Silva.
2 He's from Brazil.
3 He's the president of Brazil.

**3** c

**4**
1 Lula's family
2 Lula's education
3 Lula's career

**5**
1 False
2 True
3 False
4 False
5 True
6 True
7 False

**7** b

**8** teacher, policeman, nurse, cashier, driver, cook, cleaner, gardener, engineer

**10**
1 M
2 T
3 W
4 T
5 W
6 T
7 M
8 M
9 W
10 M

**11**
1 the nets
2 Ron and his wife
3 the crew
4 the supplies
5 the radio
6 the father and son

**12**
1 nets
2 crew
3 storm
4 sinking
5 weather forecast

**13**
1 The worst thing
2 wasn't so difficult
3 I don't think
4 The best activity
5 I don't like

**14**
1 I had a few problems
2 I didn't have enough time
3 Can we do more work on this?
4 it was a bit long for me
5 I need more
6 It's more interesting

# Unit 2

## 2A

**1**
1 desert
2 mountain
3 forest
4 village
5 church
6 lake
7 ruins
8 river
9 railway
10 beach
11 castle
12 island

**2**
1 far
2 high
3 long
4 much
5 old

**3**
1 Beijing, hotter
2 Buenos Aires, coolest
3 Beijing, hottest
4 warmer, Buenos Aires
5 wetter, Buenos Aires
6 Bergen, heaviest
7 Buenos Aires, lightest
8 Beijing, highest

**4**
1 warm
2 heaviest
3 higher
4 most uncomfortable
5 wetter
6 best

## 2B

**1**
**Opinion** lovely, pretty, beautiful, interesting, nice
**Fact** quiet, green, old, white, warm, little, grey, high, new, blue

**2**
1 beautiful
2 warm
3 quiet
4 high
5 interesting
6 lovely

**3**
1 pretty little villages
2 fine colourful forests
3 beautiful cloud-covered mountains
4 interesting old churches
5 lovely cool rivers
6 pretty white lighthouses
7 lovely green islands
8 nice clean beaches
9 fine little towns
10 interesting old ruins

**4**
1 b
2 c
3 a
4 b
5 a
6 b

## 2C

**1** cloudy, snow, storm, windy, rain, fog, sunny, hot, warm, cold

**2**
1 hottest
2 rain
3 lowest
4 wettest
5 light
6 high
7 heavy

## 2D

**1**
1 spoon
2 postcard
3 mugs
4 T-shirt
5 plate
6 rug
The word in grey is *poster*

**2**
1 Panama
2 Peru
3 Tunisia
4 Egypt
5 China
6 Austria
7 Greece

**3**
1 got
2 didn't go
3 didn't have
4 bought
5 brought
6 loved
7 left
8 took

**4**
1 Where did you get that rug?
2 Where did she buy it?
3 When did she go to Morocco?
4 Did she like it there?
5 How did she travel?
6 Did she visit the desert?

**5**
a 3
b 5
c 1
d 6
e 4
f 2

## Skills Practice

**1** b

**2**
1 November–June
2 morning
3 lower
4 higher
5 higher

**3**
a 4
b 1
c 5
d 2
e 3

**4**
1 Sun, sea, and sand
2 On your own two feet
3 Back to nature
4 Explore the past

**5**
1 Cancun, Acapulco
2 Popocatépetl
3 Izt-Popo
4 Teotihuacán, Chichén Itzá

**7**
1 1924
2 941
3 410
4 2,450
5 16 hours
6 September

**10**
1 outdoor holiday
2 spectacular scenery
3 very cold
4 long holidays

# Unit 1

1

## 1A

**1** father, daughter, husband, sister, uncle, grandmother, cousin, grandfather, aunt, brother, wife, son, mother

**2**
1 grandmother's
2 sisters'
3 father's
4 aunts'
5 brother's
6 grandfather's

**3**
1 stage name
2 first name
3 surname
4 middle name
5 nickname

## 1B

**1** **Across**
2 passport
4 envelope
7 driving licence
8 badge

**Down**
1 note
3 credit card
5 ticket
6 letter

**2** **Surname**: Winterbottom
**First name**: Wilfred
**Age**: 71
**Nationality**: English (British)
**Place of birth**: Chester
**Marital status**: single
**Job**: retired
**Interests**: travelling / collecting hats / learning languages

**3**
1 thinks
2 goes
3 remembers
4 misses
5 sleeps
6 sleeps
7 talks
8 drinks
9 dances
10 watches
11 makes
12 does
13 says
14 paints
15 feels

**4**
1 S
2 D
3 S
4 S
5 D
6 S
7 D
8 D

**6** teaches, watches, pushes, closes, kisses, dances, washes, finishes

## 1C

**1**
1 What
2 Where
3 What
4 Where
5 Who
6 How
7 Where
8 What

**2**
a 3
b 1
c 2
d 5
e 6
f 4
g 8
h 7

**3**
1 Where **are** my glasses?
2 What**'s** he doing?
He**'s** reading.
3 What **does** he do?
He**'s** a taxi driver.
4 Where **do** you live?
5 Why **are** you crying?
Because I**'m** very unhappy!
6 How **does** this work?
7 When **did** you finish school?
8 Who **did** you talk to on the phone?
9 Why **did** Tony get divorced?
I **don't** know!
10 What **was** Ibiza like?
It **was** wonderful!

## 1D

**1**
1 b
2 j
3 f
4 g
5 c
6 a
7 i
8 d
9 e
10 h

**2**
1 sounds
2 opposite
3 past
4 means
5 opposite
6 kind
7 sounds
8 past
9 opposite

**3** *Example answers*
1 See sounds the same as sea.
2 Ring means the same as call.
3 Long is the opposite of short.
4 Wrote is the past of write.
5 Salmon is a kind of fish.
6 Meet sounds the same as meat.

**4**
1 b
2 f
3 g
4 c
5 a
6 h
7 i
8 d
9 e

## Skills Practice

**1**
1 Suryono, Gunawan
2 Indrawati, Indrawan
3 Sulaemi
4 Paulus
5 Eddy, Susi

**3**
1 M, W
2 M, W
3 M
4 W
5 W

**4**
a 1
b 4
c 6
d 8
e 3
f 2
g 7
h 5

**5**
b I'm going there, too.
a Do you **live** there?
b No, I'm just visiting. I've got some **work** there.
a Oh really? **What** do you do?
b I'm an artist.
a That's interesting! **Do** you paint pictures of **people**?

**7**
1 My family
2 My job
3 My studies
4 My free time

**9**
1 False
2 True
3 False
4 True
5 False
6 False

**10**
1 the other day
2 reads it too
3 for work
4 every year
5 come to class

**11** The other day, I was talking to Jean-Jacques. He's the same age as me, but he's got a **job**. He works in a **factory** in a different part of town. He says the job isn't very interesting, but he gets **enough** money to pay for a small car. He loves taking **photographs** and he knows a lot about it. He spends a lot of his free time **visiting** new places and taking pictures. Maybe he can help me with my **new** digital **camera**.

free classes. Low Int Int. entry 1.

847/49 10 - 12 Thurs.

$6^{45}$ - $8^{30}$ Tues.

# English Result

**Pre-intermediate** Workbook Answer Key Booklet

Joe McKenna

OXFORD

# How to describe a route

# 10D

**G** *used to* **V** prepositions of direction **P** *used* = /juːzd/ or /juːst/

## A Vocabulary prepositions of direction

**1** Look at the route plan and put the sentences in order.

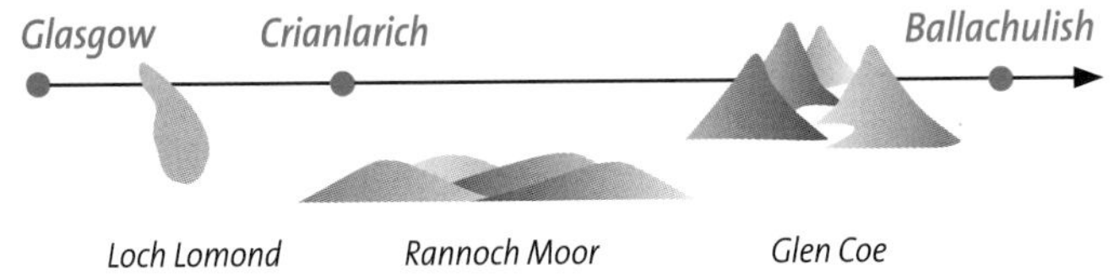


a ☐ Next you cross the wild country of Rannoch Moor, before going through dramatic Glen Coe to the sea at Ballachulish.

b ☐ Go through the town of Crianlarich and then follow the road north.

c ☐ Drive north from Glasgow, along the western side of Loch Lomond.

**2** Complete the directions with these words.

along end reach until takes

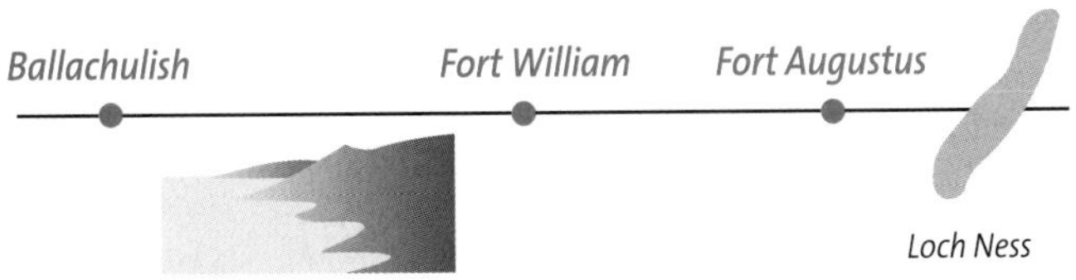


After Ballachulish, go north [1]__________ the coast [2]__________ you come to Fort William, where many people stop to visit the town. Continue on the A82, and you'll [3]__________ Fort Augustus, a small town at the south [4]__________ of Loch Ness. The whole journey [5]__________ about three hours.

## B Grammar *used to*

**3** Complete the sentences about travelling before there were cars and planes. Use *used to* and these verbs.

travel ~~walk~~ go send stay be

1 Most people *used to walk* everywhere they went.
2 Public transport ________________ much better.
3 People ________________ important news by horse.
4 People ________________ more by boat.
5 Only rich people ________________ abroad.
6 People ________________ at home much more.

**4** Rewrite the sentences with *used to*.

1 I lived in America when I was a child.
*I used to live in America when I was a child*.
2 My dad wore a tie in his last job.
____________________________.
3 As a teenager, I went to a lot of parties.
____________________________.
4 I shopped at the old market before they built the supermarket.
____________________________.
5 We bought CDs every weekend in our teenage years.
____________________________.
6 I slept until ten o'clock every morning at university.
____________________________.

## C Pronunciation *used* = /juːzd/ or /juːst/

**5** **10D.1▶** Read and listen to the sentences.

1 [A] He used a false name.
2 ☐ She used a computer to do her homework.
3 ☐ We often used to go to the beach.
4 ☐ My grandparents used to visit us every summer.
5 ☐ She used her imagination and solved the problem.
6 ☐ I used to love going to concerts.

**6** When is the pronunciation *A* /juːzd/ and when is it *B* /juːst/? Complete the boxes in 5. Write *A* or *B*.

**7** Listen again and copy the pronunciation.

**And you?** Complete the sentences.

1 When I was a small child, I used to ...
____________________________.
2 When I was a teenager, I used to ...
____________________________.
3 When we went on family holidays, we used to ...
____________________________.
4 In winter, my family used to ...
____________________________.
5 At school, my friends and I used to ...
____________________________.

**How well can you describe a route now?**
Go back to the Student's Book >> p.103 and tick ✓ the line again.

# Unit 10 Skills Practice

## A Read for detail

**1** Read the text and complete the notes.

The Tokaido (the Eastern Coast Road) is one of Japan's great traditional routes. It connected the old capital of Kyoto to the modern capital of Tokyo. For over 250 years it was the most important route in the country.

The Tokaido was about 500 kms long and the complete journey by horse took about twelve days. There were 53 post stations along the way, where people could change horses and rest. Not everyone travelled by horse, of course. In fact, most ordinary people travelled on foot. Because the route was quite safe, it became very popular. Other services soon appeared along the route: tea houses, souvenir shops, and public baths for tired travellers.

In the 19th century, important artists made drawings of famous places along the Tokaido. The drawings became popular souvenirs, similar to modern postcards. There was even a comic book about the adventures of two young troublemakers who made the complete journey along the Tokaido.

In 1889, the first Tokyo–Kyoto railway was opened. It closely followed the route of the original Tokaido, and the complete journey took only twenty hours. Modern trains do the trip in about two and a half hours. However, much of the old route still exists, and you can still walk along sections of it – if you have the time!

**Tokaido** FACT FILE

**ROUTE:**
from 1 *Kyoto*
to 2 ______

**TOTAL DISTANCE:**
3 ______

**JOURNEY TIMES:**
by horse 4 ______
by first trains 5 ______
by modern trains 6 ______

**2** Find these words in the text and match them with their meanings.

1 ☐ route
2 ☐ journey
3 ☐ ordinary
4 ☐ drawings
5 ☐ troublemaker

a a person who makes problems for other people
b travelling from one place to another
c pictures made by pens or pencils
d a way from one place to another
e not special or unusual

## B Read for detail

**3** Read the text quickly and tick ✓ the best title.

☐ Flying Is Fun
☐ Cheapest Isn't Always Best
☐ An Exciting Flight

Flying is a wonderful way to travel, until it starts going wrong. There's one flight I had a long time ago that I remember very well.

I was travelling home from India. It was the cheapest flight I could find, because I didn't have much money. We had to make several stops on the way, and one of them was in Beirut. There was nothing special about that, except that the plane broke down. They told us that we would have to wait some time for another plane to arrive. They didn't tell us just how long we would have to wait! Twelve hours in the airport! The temperatures were very high, the passengers were very tired, and children were crying all the time. And the only thing to do was watch the people in the airport.

Well, we finally got another plane, but we arrived in Prague so late that we missed all the connecting flights. So we had to spend a night in a hotel an hour's drive from the airport. Then we had a long wait again the next day to board another flight back home to Amsterdam.

I was very happy to get into the terminal building and phone home. But I wasn't so happy when I opened my suitcase at home – all the presents I brought back from India were gone. Somebody somewhere opened the bags and stole the presents. I think that was the worst part of the whole experience.

**4** Put the place names in order.

☐ Amsterdam ☐ Beirut
☐ Prague ☐ India

**5** Write *true* or *false*.

1 The plane broke down in Prague. ______
2 The weather in Beirut was very hot. ______
3 The passenger had to spend a whole day in Beirut. ______
4 The passenger lost things from her bags. ______

## C Listen to a holiday experience

6 **105.1▶** Listen to a woman talking about her trip to South Africa and put these place names in order.

- ☐ Gold Reef City
- ☐ Soweto
- ☐ Pilanesberg
- ☐ Muldersdrift
- ☐ Apartheid Museum

7 Match the phrases with the places in exercise 6.

a really interesting ________
b just like on TV ________
c isn't much cheaper ________
d a really exciting place ________
e we took a lot of photos ________

8 Put the first speaker's questions in order.

a ☐ Did you bring any gold back with you?
b ☐ And where else did you go?
c ☐ Did you see any animals?
d ☐ Where did you stay?
e ☐ What was that like?

## D Write a travel diary

9 Complete the text with these phrases.

we didn't visit it   we haven't been there yet   we've already seen   we've just come back   we've also

*This is our first day in Edinburgh. It's very windy, but it hasn't rained very much. 1________ the castle, and Lina thinks it's better from the outside than the inside. It's also a bit expensive, and you can't visit all of it. But the views of the city are wonderful. 2________ walked along the Royal Mile. It's a street which goes from the castle to the Palace of Holyroodhouse. The palace was closed, so 3________, but we did some shopping on the Mile. It's full of souvenir shops, and they're not too expensive. 4________ to get changed and go out for supper. Tonight we're going to a traditional dance party, and tomorrow we're going to have a picnic in the Botanical Gardens. 5________, and Lina really wants to go.*

10 Answer the questions about the text.

1 What city are they visiting? ________
2 What is the weather like? ________
3 What two places have they already visited? ________
4 What do they like about the city? ________
5 What don't they like about it? ________
6 What are they going to do tomorrow? ________

11 Now imagine you are on holiday. Complete the notes in the table.

| | |
|---|---|
| Name of the city | |
| What's it like? | |
| I've already visited ... | |
| I like ... | |
| I don't like ... | |
| I'm going to visit ... | |

12 Write about your first day in your travel diary.

________
________
________
________

13 Check your writing. Have you used the words *already*, *just*, or *yet*?

**Now try the Self check on** >> p.85.

# How to describe symptoms

**v** symptoms of illness

11A

## A Vocabulary symptoms of illness

**1** Put the letters in order and complete the sentences.

1 A man felt sick so he went to the *doctor's*. (otdorcs')
2 He told the doctor his ________. (moptssmy)
3 He said he had a bad ________. (gouch)
4 He said he had a ________. (chasmot each)
5 He said he had a ________. (rose hattor)
6 He said he had ________. (chabcake)
7 He said he had a ________. (adhhecae)
8 The doctor took his ________. (retmtprauee)
9 He gave him an ________. (sapinir)

**2** Match the words 1–6 and their meanings a–f.

1 [c] another word for 'pill'
2 [ ] when a woman is expecting a baby
3 [ ] the feeling when pain goes away
4 [ ] the correct quantity of medicine to take
5 [ ] the paper you give to the chemist for your medicine
6 [ ] the medicine is good before this time

a prescription
b dose
c ~~tablet~~
d pregnancy
e expiry date
f relief

**3** Put the sentences in order.

1 feel you do how
________?
2 matter the what's
________?
3 it you for have anything taken
________?
4 well soon get
________!
5 better you lot a look
________!

**4** Complete the conversation with the sentences from exercise 3.

**A** Hello, Fran! You don't look too good.
[1] ________?
**B** You're right. I feel awful. I didn't sleep well last night and I've got a terrible headache.
**A** Oh dear! [2] ________?
**B** I took some pills this morning, but I don't notice any difference.
**A** Well, try some of this. My grandmother recommends it.
**B** Mmm, it's got a funny taste!

*Ten minutes later*

**A** [3] ________?
**B** I feel nice and warm inside! What is that?
**A** I don't really know. Well, I think
[4] ________! Take some home with you. Take a big cup of it after meals.
**B** I will. And thanks!
**A** OK! And [5] ________!

**How well can you describe symptoms now?**
Go back to the Student's Book >> p.107 and tick ✓ the line again.

# How to say how people appear

**G** action or state verbs **P** unstressed words

11B

## A Grammar action or state verbs

**1** Underline the correct words.

'He [1]stands/is standing next to a desk. Yes, that's it. And he [2]writes/is writing on a piece of paper. I [3]don't know/am not knowing what is on the paper – I can't read it! Oh, just a minute. He [4]seems/is seeming to be angry. Yes, now he [5]looks/is looking to the left. I [6]think/am thinking there's someone in the next room. Yes, he [7]moves/is moving his arm. Maybe he [8]wants/is wanting something. Oh, and now he [9]watches/is watching TV. It's 9 p.m. [10]Do you remember/Are you remembering what programme is on at 9 p.m.?'

**2** Complete the dialogue. Use the present simple or present continuous.

**A** Who's that man over there?
**B** Where?
**A** The one in the blue suit. He [1]*'s sitting*______ (sit) near the window.
**B** Oh yes. Erm, I [2]__________ (think) he works in the sales department, but I [3]__________ (not remember) his name.
**A** He [4]__________ (seem) to be waiting for someone.
**B** What makes you say that?
**A** Because he [5]__________ (look) at his watch.
**B** Hmm. Talking of the time, I have to leave – I [6]__________ (not want) to be home late. Anyway, didn't you have a meeting today or something?
**A** My goodness! You're right. I need to see somebody called Winkelstein. He [7]__________ (prepare) a trip to Japan, and [8]__________ (want) some help.
**B** Winkelstein? That's his name!
**A** Whose name?
**B** The man over there at the window! Hey – it must be you he [9]__________ (wait) for!
**A** Oh no!
**B** Run, John, run! I'll see you later!

## B Pronunciation unstressed words

**3** **11B.1▶** The red words are stressed. Listen and notice how the other (unstressed) words sound.

She's looking at the man's face in the mirror
He's looking at the traffic in front of him
Then he sees her in the mirror and smiles
She smiles at him too
The light changes to green
And they drive off in different directions

**4** Listen again and practise saying the lines. Copy the pronunciation of the unstressed words.

**How well can you say how people appear now?**
Go back to the Student's Book >> p.109 and tick ✓ the line again.

# How to give your ideas

# 11C

**G** verb + infinitive (with *to*) **V** verbs for giving ideas **P** stress in two-syllable verbs and nouns

## A Vocabulary verbs for giving ideas

**1** Underline the correct verb.

1 'I've got the passport and tickets. Let's go!'
She's forgotten / tried / decided to travel abroad.

2 'What's the matter with this car? It won't start!'
He promised / agreed / tried to start the car.

3 'I think it's better to leave early.'
I pretend / prefer / refuse to leave early.

4 'Don't worry – I'll wait for you.'
She tried / forgot / promised to wait.

5 'I'm not going to leave!'
He tried / forgot / refused to leave.

6 'All right. Let's talk about it.'
She agreed / hoped / planned to talk.

7 'Ohh, I feel terrible. I think I'm going to die.'
He pretended / refused / agreed to be sick.

8 'I didn't take the letter with me – I didn't remember!'
She tried / forgot / preferred to post the letter.

9 'How much does that cost?'
He agreed / wanted / planned to know the price.

## B Grammar verb + infinitive (with *to*)

**2** Put the second sentences in order.

1 Oh no! I've left my umbrella at home!
umbrella forgot she her take to
*She forgot to take her umbrella*.

2 OK, I'll come and visit you at the weekend.
the promised me weekend visit he to at
____________________.

3 Can I go home early today?
home wants early he go today to
____________________.

4 Yes, that's it! I'm going to move to Paris.
Paris move she to to decided
____________________.

5 Six o'clock is a better time for me to arrive.
prefers o'clock arrive six to at he
____________________.

**3** Rewrite the sentences. Use infinitives.

1 I'm sorry, but I can't take your money.
She refused *to take his money*.

2 All right, let's meet at the station.
We agreed ____________________.

3 We've booked a holiday flight for April.
They're planning ____________________ in April.

4 I've studied really hard for this exam!
She's hoping ____________________.

5 There's a problem with the door! I can't open it!
He tried ____________________.

## C Pronunciation stress in two-syllable verbs and nouns

**4** **11C.1▸** Listen and underline the word with different stress.

| | | | |
|---|---|---|---|
| 1 | agree | reason | pretend |
| 2 | feelings | suggest | topic |
| 3 | lifestyle | singer | decide |
| 4 | become | refuse | finger |
| 5 | passport | exam | prefer |
| 6 | compare | problem | promise |
| 7 | forget | answer | career |

**5** Listen again and practise saying the words.

**How well can you give your ideas now?**
Go back to the Student's Book >> p.111 and tick ✓ the line again.

# How to say how something was done

**11D**

**G** past passive **V** the face

## A Vocabulary the face

1 Complete the crossword.

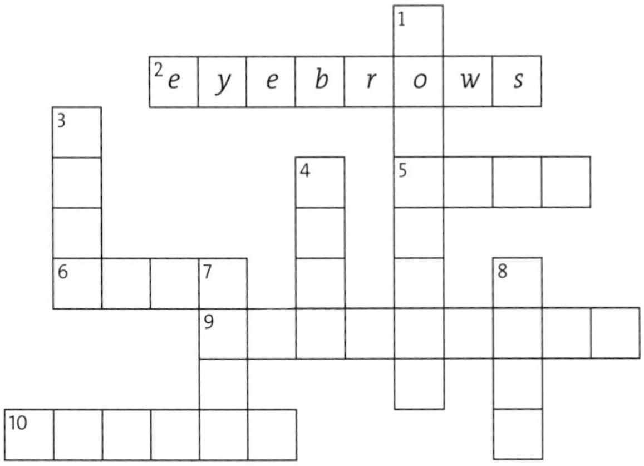


**Across**
2 This is the name for the hair just above your eyes.
5 You've got two, and you use them for listening.
6 This covers your whole body.
9 These fine hairs protect your eyes from dust.
10 These turn red when you're very warm.

**Down**
1 This is the highest part of your face.
3 You've got two, and you use them for kissing.
4 You've got one, and it's in the middle of your face.
7 This connects your head to your shoulders.
8 This is the lowest part of your face.

## B Grammar past passive

2 Underline the correct words in the text.

The Taj Mahal [1]built/was built by the Emperor Shah Jahan in memory of his wife Mumtaz Mahal. Construction work began in 1632, and the monument [2]completed/was completed in 1648. The Taj Mahal [3]did not design/was not designed by one person alone: a team of 30 to 40 people from several different countries [4]worked/were worked on the project over a long period of time. The physical work [5]did/was done by about twenty thousand workers, who [6]hired/were hired in northern India. Special materials [7]brought/were brought from all over India, and even from abroad. The monument's famous white marble blocks [8]transported/were transported by elephants.

3 Complete the text with the verbs in the past simple passive.

### The Stone of Destiny

The Stone of Destiny [1] *was used* (use) for centuries to crown the kings of Scotland. In 1296, the stone [2]__________ (take) to London by the English army, and it [3]__________ (put) under the English king's throne. The stone [4]__________ (keep) there for 700 years. But one day in 1950, the stone [5]__________ (steal). It [6]__________ (not find) until four months later. The thieves [7]__________ (not arrest) because they [8]__________ (never discover). The stone broke in two pieces and so it [9]__________ (repair) before going back to London. Finally in 1996, the stone [10]__________ (return) to Scotland. And you can see it today in Edinburgh Castle.

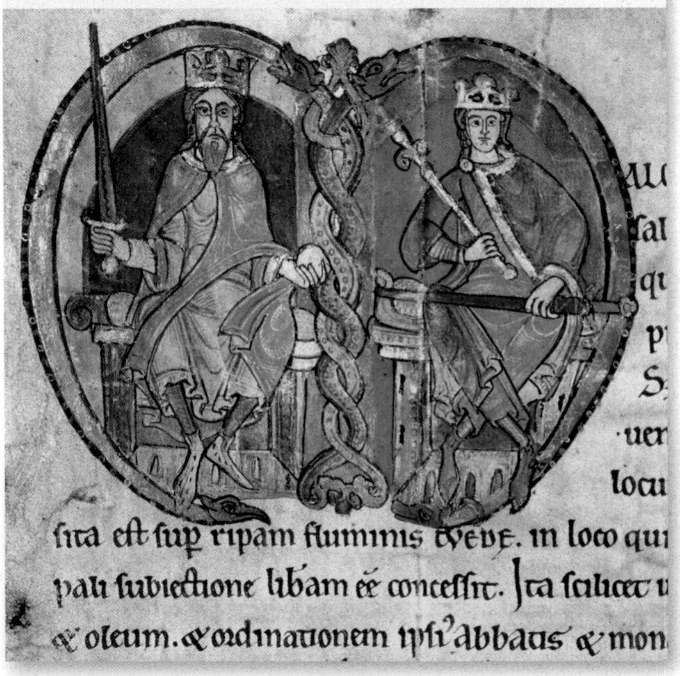

How well can you say how something was done now?
Go back to the Student's Book >> p.113 and tick ✓ the line again.

# Unit 11 Skills Practice

## A Read instructions

**1** Read the text quickly. Who are these instructions mainly for?

a ☐ doctors
b ☐ nurses
c ☐ chemists
d ☐ patients

**a** keep your medicines in wet places, like the kitchen or bathroom.

**b** tell the doctor, nurse, or chemist if you are allergic to any kind of medicine.

**c** keep your medicines locked away and out of reach of children.

**d** tell your doctor if your medicines give you any problems.

**e** take anyone else's medicines, or give yours to anyone.

**f** read the label and follow the instructions so you don't take the wrong dose.

**g** stop taking your medicine or change the dose on your own.

**h** check the expiry date on your medicines, and take out-of-date medicines back to the chemist's.

**i** put your medicine in different containers because somebody could take the wrong medicine by mistake.

**j** skip doses. Ask the doctor what to do if you forget a dose.

**k** keep all medicines in a cool, dry, dark place – for example, in a cupboard.

**l** take medicines with alcoholic drinks.

**2** Read the text more carefully. Decide if the instructions are things you should do (*Do*), or shouldn't do (*Don't*).

✓ Do ... b ☐ ☐ ☐ ☐ ☐ ☐
✗ Don't ... a ☐ ☐ ☐ ☐ ☐ ☐

**3** Look at the highlighted phrases in the text. Read the sentences around them and match them with their meanings.

1 alone / without help ____________
2 in a place that you close with a key ____________
3 without planning to do it ____________
4 too far away to touch ____________
5 too old to be useful ____________

## B Read for general meaning

**4** Match the notes with the people who wrote them.

1 ☐ girlfriend 2 ☐ mother 3 ☐ travel agent 4 ☐ flatmate 5 ☐ doctor

**a**

West Side Health Clinic
27, Skid Row, York

Your next appointment: Wed. 24th May

*If you are unable to attend, please notify the clinic as soon as possible.*

**b**

Dinner Wednesday?
How about that romantic Italian place?
xxx

**c**

*Tom, your father's got a meeting in York today. He was thinking of having lunch with you. Will you be free at lunchtime? It would be a good idea for you to have a proper meal. I still think you were too thin the last time you came home. Love,*

**d**

Easy Trips PLC, 14 Swindon Place.
Tel 020 946 5027

Dear Mr Davis,

Please find enclosed your train tickets. Kindly check details of dates and times. If you have any queries, please call us at the above telephone number.

Yours sincerely

**e**

Tom,

Can you do me a favour? I'm going home for the weekend, and I don't want to take the cat with me. Can you feed her for me? There's a tin of cat food in the cupboard under the sink.

Buy you a beer when I get back!

**5** Match the highlighted words and phrases with their meanings.

1 help me ____________
2 questions ____________
3 good, healthy ____________
4 tell, inform ____________

## C Listen for key words

6 Read the key words for four news reports. What do you think happened?

| a | b |
|---|---|
| paintings<br>museum<br>police | president<br>hospital<br>doctors |
| **c** | **d** |
| car<br>accident<br>lorry<br>motorway | prison<br>Oscar<br>paparazzi<br>nose |

7 11S.1 Listen and check. Match the reports and the key words.

8 Listen again and answer the questions.

1 How many times has the president been in hospital? ________

2 How many paintings were stolen? ________

3 How many paparazzi were there? ________

4 How many people were in the car? ________

9 Check the audio script on >> p.94.

## D Write an accident report

10 Complete the text with these words.

cars date and time drivers accident place clearly finally

1 ______________ Tuesday, 7th January, 11.15 a.m.

2 ______________ Market St.

3 ______________ red Honda Civic ZAP 1T; blue Ford Focus, AFO 3DT.

4 ______________ Mr J. Harris; Mr S. Parker.

Details of 5 ______________

I was waiting at the traffic lights when a car came from behind and hit mine! I looked in the mirror and saw the driver talking on his mobile phone. That is illegal in this country! 6 ______________, he wasn't paying attention. I got out of the car to talk to the other driver, but he refused to listen. 7 ______________ I called the police. The back of my car is badly damaged and I had to go to the doctor about my neck. The doctor thinks I'll have to stay at home for about a month.

11 Write an accident report about the pictures. Imagine you are the cyclist. Try to include some of the words in exercise 10.

______________________________

______________________________

______________________________

______________________________

______________________________

______________________________

Now try the Self check on >> p.86.

# How to ask people to do things

**G** gerund or infinitive **V** polite requests **P** polite requests

12A

## A Grammar gerund or infinitive

**1** Underline the correct words.

1 She ran because she didn't want arriving / to arrive late.
2 That's OK. I don't mind waiting / to wait.
3 I'm very happy that you agreed coming / to come.
4 Do you enjoy to listen / listening to classical music?
5 I'd like going / to go, but I really have to study.
6 Tom refuses playing / to play with the other children.
7 She promised sending / to send me the book.
8 If you can't talk now, I don't mind to call / calling back.

**2** Complete the sentences with the correct form of these verbs.

be buy catch eat have to sit ~~stand~~ travel watch

1 I hate *standing* in long queues at the airport.
2 I enjoy __________ things at duty-free shops.
3 I don't like __________ go through the security checks.
4 I refuse __________ meals in the airport because they're very expensive!
5 I didn't really want __________ by plane, but I promised __________ at my niece's wedding.
6 I love __________ the clouds below us.
7 I decided __________ near the front this time because I need __________ a connecting flight in only 40 minutes.

## B Vocabulary polite requests

**3** Put the requests in order.

1 would this to way you come like
*Would you like to come this way*?
2 number giving would me mind you phone your
____________________?
3 my with you bags help could me
____________________?
4 name sign to you like would your
____________________?
5 would back you minutes mind five calling in
____________________?
6 a you me taxi call for could
____________________?

**4** Match the answers with the questions in exercise 3.

a ☐ Yes, of course. Let me carry them.
b ☐ All right. It's 647 9364.
c ☐ No problem – I'll try later.
d [1] Yes, of course. Where are we going?
e ☐ OK. Where do I sign?
f ☐ Yes, sir. To the airport?

## C Pronunciation polite requests

**5** **12A.1** ▸ Listen and repeat the requests in exercise 3. Copy the intonation.

**And you?** Complete the sentences.

1 I love ____________________.
2 I don't mind ____________________.
3 I hate ____________________.
4 I would love ____________________.
5 I need ____________________.
6 I enjoy ____________________.

**How well can you ask people to do things now?**
Go back to the Student's Book >> p.117 and tick ✓ the line again.

# How to describe a festival

# 12B

G indefinite pronouns / adverbs V festivals and celebrations P stress in words ending *-tion*

## A Grammar indefinite pronouns / adverbs

**1** Match the sentences 1–8 and the responses a–h.

1 [d] There's someone at the door!
2 [ ] Is there no one I can talk to?
3 [ ] Does anyone have the time?
4 [ ] Have you seen John anywhere?
5 [ ] So where **is** Timbuktu?
6 [ ] I've got something in my eye.
7 [ ] Will everyone please stop talking?
8 [ ] Is there anything I can do to help?

a Isn't he in his room?
b Could you set the table?
c Why? What's the matter?
d ~~Well, go and answer it!~~
e Yes, it looks like a hair.
f Talk to me – I'm listening!
g Somewhere in Africa.
h It's half past three.

**2** Underline the correct words in the conversation on a school trip.

**Teacher** Has [1] anyone / anything / anywhere seen Thomas? I can't find him [2] anyone / anything / anywhere!

**Children** There's [3] someone / anyone / no one on the bus, sir!

**Teacher** Yes, that's him! Tell him to get off the bus. [4] No one / Someone / Everyone gets on the bus until we're all ready. Now, has [5] no one / someone / everyone put their bags in the bus?

**Children** Not yet, sir!

**Teacher** Come on then! I want [6] someone / anyone / everyone ready in ten minutes! Charles! Did you say [7] something / nothing / everything?

**Tom** Just a question, sir. Clara says we're going to stop [8] somewhere / nowhere / anywhere for lunch. Is that right?

**Teacher** No, it's not right. There's [9] somewhere / nowhere / anywhere interesting to stop, so you'll have lunch on the bus. I told you to bring sandwiches!

**Sophie** Mark says he hasn't got [10] something / nothing / anything to eat, sir.

**Teacher** Well, you'll have to share with him, then.

**Sophie** What?

## B Vocabulary festivals and celebrations

**3** Match these words with the meanings.

a ceremony a competition
a colourful celebration traditional costumes

1 a formal event with special actions – a wedding, for example ______________
2 the special clothes of a country ______________
3 a kind of game where the winner gets a prize ______________
4 a kind of big, noisy party with lots of bright, interesting things to see ______________

## C Pronunciation stress in words ending *-tion*

**4** Underline the word with a different number of syllables.

| | | | |
|---|---|---|---|
| 1 | tradition | position | station |
| 2 | information | imagination | destination |
| 3 | presentation | congratulations | pronunciation |
| 4 | celebration | location | competition |
| 5 | connection | direction | invitation |

**5** 12B.1 ▸ Listen and check.

**6** Listen again and repeat. Practise the stress.

| **And you?** Answer the questions. |
|---|
| 1 Name three tropical countries. |
| 2 Do you enjoy any sports competitions? Which ones? |
| 3 What traditional costumes does your country have? |
| 4 Do you know anyone who's been on a camel ride? |
| 5 Have you ever seen an elephant? Where? |
| 6 Are there any lively celebrations in your town? When? |

**How well can you describe a festival now?**
Go back to the Student's Book >> p.119 and tick ✓ the line again.

# How to accept and refuse invitations

# 12C

**G** future forms **V** going out phrases **P** *yes* or *yes, but* intonation

## A Grammar future forms

**1** Underline the correct words.

1 A Would you like to order?
  B Yes! I think I'll have / I'm having the fish.
2 A What will you do / are you doing tonight?
  B I haven't got anything planned.
3 A This bag is so heavy.
  B Give it to me. I'll carry / I'm carrying it.
4 A Have you got any plans for the weekend?
  B Yes, we'll go / we're going camping.
5 A See you on Monday!
  B No – I'll fly / I'm flying to Holland on Monday!
6 A What's that you're eating?
  B Snails. Try them – you're going to / you'll like them!
7 A Oh, please come tonight!
  B OK, I'll come / I'm going to come.
8 A Where are you going on holiday?
  B I don't know yet. I'm deciding / I'm going to decide next month.

**2** Put the conversation in order.

A [1] Are you busy this weekend?
A ☐ Will you phone me when you get to the top?
A ☐ Fun? Isn't it a bit dangerous?
A ☐ Have you done it before?

B ☐ Oh, stop worrying. I promise I'll be careful.
B ☐ I'm not going to take my phone! It could get broken!
B ☐ Yes, I am, actually. I'm going rock climbing.
B ☐ No, but I think it'll be fun.

## B Vocabulary going out phrases

**3** Put the letters in order and complete the invitations and responses.

1 ☐ Are you doing *anything* tomorrow? (ynnaight)
2 ☐ Do you ________ going out for a meal? (cynaf)
3 ☐ How ________ going camping for the weekend? (otuba)
4 ☐ ________ you like to watch the football tonight? (dulow)
5 ☐ Are you ________ this weekend? Do you want to go skiing? (ybsu)

a I'd ________ not. They say there'll be rain – and anyway I haven't got a tent. (rhreat)
b ________ much, really. Why? (gonthin)
c I'd ________ not to. I don't have enough money for the hotel. (refper)
d ________ some other time! I've got an exam tomorrow morning. (ameby)
e Yes, I'd love a Chinese! ________'s meet at your flat at 7.30. (elt)

**4** Match the invitations 1–5 and responses a–e in exercise 3.

## C Pronunciation *yes* or *yes, but* intonation

**5** 12C.1 ▸ Listen and tick ✓ the ending you expect to hear.

1 That's very kind of you ...
  ☐ but I'm afraid I can't.
  ☐ Thanks!
2 I think that's great ...
  ☐ but sorry, I can't.
  ☐ I'll see you tonight.
3 That's a lovely idea ...
  ☐ but I've already got plans. Sorry.
  ☐ Where shall we meet?
4 Oh I'd love to ...
  ☐ but really, I can't.
  ☐ What time shall we meet?
5 I think that's a great idea ...
  ☐ but I haven't got time. Sorry!
  ☐ I'd love to!

**6** 12C.2 ▸ Listen and check.

**7** Listen again and practise the different intonation.

**How well can you accept and refuse invitations now?**
Go back to the Student's Book >> p.121 and tick ✓ the line again.

# How to talk about imagined situations

**G** 2nd conditional

## A Grammar 2nd conditional

**1** Match 1–8 with a–h.

1 [e] If I knew French, ...
2 [ ] If I could go back to school, ...
3 [ ] If our children were older, ...
4 [ ] If houses were cheaper, ...
5 [ ] If I had three months' holiday every year, ...
6 [ ] If she was rich, ...
7 [ ] If we had his photograph, ...
8 [ ] If they lived closer, ...

a we could help the children buy their first one.
b she would buy a Ferrari.
c I'd study biology.
d we'd remember him better.
e ~~I'd move to Paris.~~
f they could go on holiday with their friends.
g I'd spend two of them travelling.
h we'd visit them more often.

**2** Complete the second conditional sentences with the correct form of the verbs in brackets.

1 If we *recycled* more paper, we *would save* more trees. (recycle, save)
2 If we ________ less pollution, people ________ longer. (make, live)
3 If we ________ our rubbish in the bin, the streets ________ cleaner. (put, be)
4 If people ________ more natural food, they ________ healthier. (eat, be)
5 If everybody ________ some lights, we ________ less energy. (turn off, use)
6 If we all ________ public transport, we ________ to work faster. (use, get)

**3** Put the sentences in order.

1 would I world visit in every the country
If I could, *I would visit every country in the world*.
2 would car rich you buy a I new
If I were ________________.
3 go machine the to would I future
If I had a time ________________.
4 me her marry I say would to 'yes'
If she asked ________________.
5 I animal would be whale blue a
If I were an ________________.
6 me tell he would me loved
If he really ________________.

**And you?** Complete the sentences.

1 If people read more books,
________________.
2 If we all spoke the same language,
________________.
3 If we all drove more carefully,
________________.
4 My job would be easier if
________________.
5 Children would be happier if
________________.
6 My town would be a better place if
________________.

**How well can you talk about imagined situations now?**
Go back to the Student's Book >> p.123 and tick ✓ the line again.

# Unit 12 Skills Practice

## A Read a festival leaflet

**1** Read the text quickly. Match the headings with the paragraphs.

How do I get there? What happens at the festival? Where can I stay? Where can I get tickets? What **is** the Edinburgh Festival? When is it on?

1 ______________________________?

**THE EDINBURGH INTERNATIONAL FESTIVAL** was set up in 1947, just after the Second World War. The idea was – and still is – to bring together different countries in a celebration of their cultures. It's probably the only place where you can see Japanese theatre, African dancing, Peruvian music, Italian opera, and British military bands in the same week!

2 ______________________________?

**THE OFFICIAL FESTIVAL** offers opera, concerts, theatre, and dance performances by international companies. These companies are specially invited by the festival organizers.

**THE 'ALTERNATIVE' FESTIVAL** (The Fringe) provides literally hundreds of performances of all kinds of music, dance, theatre, comedy, etc. both indoors and outdoors, depending on weather conditions. Anyone can take part in the Fringe Festival.

3 ______________________________?

**THE FESTIVAL** is celebrated every year during the last three weeks of August. It closes with an open-air fireworks concert in the castle gardens.

4 ______________________________?

**BY AIR:** Edinburgh has an international airport with direct flights from many European capitals. There are also hourly flights from London and connections from other UK airports.

**BY TRAIN:** from London King's Cross to Edinburgh Waverley. Also from Glasgow.

**BY CAR:** Take the A1/M1 north from London. It takes between five and six hours.

5 ______________________________?

**THE CITY OF EDINBURGH** offers everything from five-star hotels to youth hostels and campsites. The most important thing is to book early because the festival period is the busiest time of the year in the city.

6 ______________________________?

**ONLINE:** www.eif.co.uk and www.edfringe.com
**BY PHONE:** (0044) 131 473 2000
**BY FAX:** (0044) 131 473 2003
**IN PERSON:** The Hub, Castlehill, Edinburgh EH1 2NE

**2** Read the text more carefully. Write *true* or *false*.

1 The Edinburgh International Festival is only for music. *False*
2 The Festival is over 50 years old. ______
3 The Festival takes place in the spring. ______
4 Anyone can take part in the Official Festival. ______
5 The Festival ends with a fireworks concert. ______
6 To get there, you can only fly via London. ______
7 There is no cheap accommodation. ______
8 You have to go to Edinburgh to buy tickets. ______

**3** Find words in the text with these meanings.

1 (para 1) to start an organization ______
2 (para 2) shows in front of an audience ______
3 (para 3) things that explode in the sky ______
4 (para 4) something that happens every sixty minutes ______

**4** Now check in your dictionary. Add the words to your vocabulary notebook. Don't forget to test yourself on the words from earlier units.

## B Read bills and tickets

**5** Complete the diary with the missing information.

orchestra dance show visit art gallery dinner see a film

| **THURSDAY 16** | |
|---|---|
| *p.m.* | 1 ______ |
| **FRIDAY 17** | |
| *3.00* | 2 ______ |
| *7.30* | 3 ______ |
| **SATURDAY 18** | |
| *1.00* | 4 ______ |
| *6.00* | 5 ______ |

USHER HALL EDINBURGH
*Top Class Productions presents*
Beethoven's Ninth Symphony
Chicago Philharmonic Orchestra
Fri. 17 August 2007 – 7.30 p.m.
Seat No. K46
PLEASE NO MOBILE PHONES

Phuket Thai Restaurant
PHUKET THAI RESTAURANT
64 Queen St. Edinburgh
Total ............................ £31.00
VAT incl.
18.8.06 – 13.00
We hope you enjoyed your meal

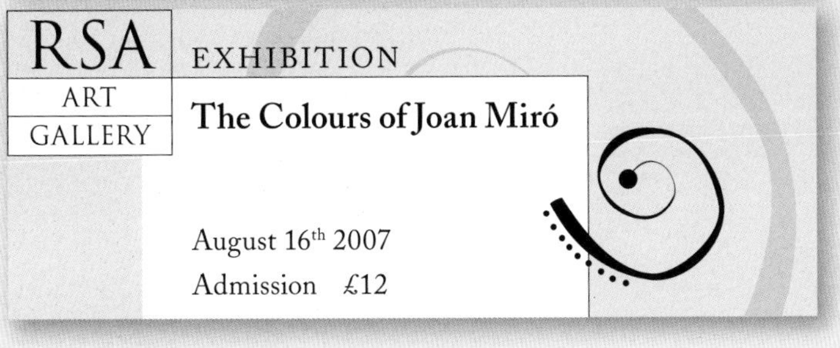


**6** Find abbreviations for these words.

1 Friday ____________ 4 Street ____________
2 Saturday ____________ 5 number ____________
3 August ____________ 6 included ____________

## C Listen for general meaning

**7** **12S.1▸** Listen to the conversation. What are the women discussing?

a ☐ two men they like
b ☐ two men they don't like
c ☐ two men they don't know

**8** Listen again carefully and write the names *Linda*, *Sasha*, *Marco*, or *Rudiger*.

1 ____________ likes Marco.
2 ____________ prefers Rudiger.
3 ____________ has got blue eyes.
4 ____________ is too quiet.
5 ____________ has got a lovely smile.
6 ____________ is going out with Linda for a drink.

**9** Check your answers in the audio script on >> p.94.

## D Write a letter to a friend

**10** Complete the letter with these phrases.

and things like that anyway ~~hi, how are you?~~
you're OK see you you'd love it here it's like

*Dear Sasha,*

*1 Hi, how are you? I hope 2 ____________ and still enjoying the wonderful British weather. Or maybe you'd prefer to be back in freezing Kiev!*

*3 ____________, here we are in Erfurt, in the heart of Germany. This place is amazing! 4 ____________ travelling back 500 years. There's an old bridge with houses on it, in the middle of the medieval town. And a big Gothic cathedral where they have lots of different festivals 5 ____________.*

*Rudiger's family are very nice, but I get on better with his university friends. There are Erasmus students here from all over Europe, and the atmosphere is great! 6 ____________!*

*Why don't you get Marco to take you on a trip to Italy?*

*7 ____________ when I get back,*

*Love,*

*Linda.*

**11** Think of a place you have visited. Make notes in the table.

| |
|---|
| Name of the place |
| What is special about it? What is it famous for? |
| What would your friend like / not like about this place? |
| Make a suggestion to your friend |

**12** Now write your own letter. Use your notes from exercise 11.

______________________________________
______________________________________
______________________________________
______________________________________
______________________________________

**13** Check your letter. Has it got any of the phrases from the letter in exercise 10?

Now try the Self check on >> p.87.

# Unit 1 Self check

1

## Grammar

**1** Tick ✓ or correct the sentences in the dialogues.

1 **A** What do you doing now?
**B** I playing a computer game.

2 **A** How is your boss like?
**B** I not know her. She's new.

3 **A** Where does she come from?
**B** She come from Switzerland.

**2** Underline the correct words to complete the text.

In Spanish-speaking [1]country / countries / country's, most [2]children / childrens / children's use the surnames of both their [3]parent's / parents / parents'. For example, Gabriel García Márquez's [4]father / father's / fathers' surname was García. His [5]mother / mothers / mother's surname was Márquez.

## Vocabulary

**3** Match the opposites.

1 ☐ father — a sister
2 ☐ brother — b aunt
3 ☐ husband — c mother
4 ☐ uncle — d daughter
5 ☐ son — e wife

**4** Decide if the underlined word is a noun or a verb.

1 Luke is going to the match tomorrow.
2 The train leaves at ten to five.
3 Carla loves going to the park in winter.
4 Everyone thinks he is an excellent cook.
5 Tina books the hotels when we go on holiday.

## Pronunciation

**5** Complete the table with these words.

~~teaches~~ goes dances kisses makes pushes plays washes likes

| ● | ●• |
|---|---|
| | *teaches* |

**Check your answers on >> p.88.**

**What are you going to do now?**

a Nothing. I'm happy.
b Revise grammar / vocabulary / pronunciation and try again.
c Ask another student / my teacher for help.

**To revise go to ...**
**Student's Book** Review >> p.15 Grammar Bank >> p.136
**Workbook** >> pp.4–7 **www.oup.com/elt/result**

## Reading

Read these texts again.
**Workbook** >> p.8 exercise 1
**Workbook** >> p.9 exercise 7

**How confident are you?**
I can understand ...
☐ some words
☐ with help
☐ when I read again
☐ everything

## Listening

Listen to this audio again.
**Workbook** >> p.8 audio script **1S.1**▶

**How confident are you?**
I can understand ...
☐ some words
☐ with help
☐ when I listen again
☐ everything

## Writing

Do this writing exercise again.
**Workbook** >> p.9 exercise 12

**How confident are you?**
I can write ...
☐ with help
☐ on my own
☐ with some mistakes
☐ with no mistakes

**What are you going to do now?**
a Nothing. I'm happy.
b Ask my teacher for help.
c Practise my reading / listening / writing.

**To practise go to ...**
**Student's Book** >> pp.6–14
**Workbook** >> pp.8–9
**MultiRom** Listening section
**www.oup.com/elt/result**

# Unit 2 Self check

2

## Grammar

**1** Match the questions and answers. There are two extra sentences.

1 ☐ Where did you get that T-shirt?
2 ☐ Where did she get it?
3 ☐ What did she do?
4 ☐ Did she enjoy it?

a She gave English classes.
b I did get it.
c My sister gave it to me.
d She sold it in a market.
e Yes, she did.
f Panama. She worked there.

**2** Put the words in brackets in the correct place.

1 I want to go on a nice holiday to Chile. (long)
2 There are some old forests and amazing waterfalls. (lovely)
3 They also have lots of pretty villages. (little)
4 And I want to go swimming in their blue lakes. (beautiful)

## Vocabulary

**3** Underline the best word.

1 We're going on a day journey / trip to Snowdon.
2 The train fare / cost is £20.
3 Where is the tourist / tourism information office?
4 How much are the round / around trip tickets?
5 Can I have a one distance / way ticket, please?

**4** Complete the sentences with these words.

snow heat storm snowy stormy hot

1 I put the air conditioning on because I'm very ________.
2 There was a lot of ________ on the mountains – it was perfect for skiing!
3 In summer it's 35° in the city. I hate it because I don't like the ________.
4 The weekend was very ________. We had wind and rain all the time.
5 We have lovely ________ weather in winter. Everything is white.
6 The weatherman said there will be a terrible ________ tomorrow.

## Pronunciation

**5** Say the phrases aloud. Complete the table.

1 lovely quiet beaches
2 fine old trees
3 pretty little islands
4 beautiful colourful villages
5 nice blue lakes
6 interesting African animals

| ● ● ● | ●• ●• ●• | ●•• ●•• ●•• |
|---|---|---|
| | | |

Check your answers on >> p.88.

What are you going to do now?

a Nothing. I'm happy.
b Revise grammar / vocabulary / pronunciation and try again.
c Ask another student / my teacher for help.

**To revise go to ...**
**Student's Book** Review >> p.25 Grammar Bank >> p.137
**Workbook** >> pp.10–13 **www.oup.com/elt/result**

## Reading

Read these texts again.
**Workbook** >> p.14 exercise 4
**Workbook** >> p.15 exercise 7

**How confident are you?**
I can understand ...

☐ some words
☐ with help
☐ when I read again
☐ everything

## Listening

Listen to this audio again.
**Workbook** >> p.14 audio script **2S.1**

**How confident are you?**
I can understand ...

☐ some words
☐ with help
☐ when I listen again
☐ everything

## Writing

Do this writing exercise again.
**Workbook** >> p.15 exercise 12

**How confident are you?**
I can write ...

☐ with help
☐ on my own
☐ with some mistakes
☐ with no mistakes

What are you going to do now?

a Nothing. I'm happy.
b Ask my teacher for help.
c Practise my reading / listening / writing.

**To practise go to ...**
**Student's Book** >> pp.16–24
**Workbook** >> pp.14–15
**MultiRom** Listening section
**www.oup.com/elt/result**

# Unit 3 Self check

3

## Grammar

**1** Underline the correct words to complete the email.

Hi Lukas

They say the weather [1]can / is going to be good on Saturday. Anni and I are thinking of going rock climbing in Snowdonia. [2]Can / Could you climb (or [3]do / would you like to try)? The bus leaves at 9.30. We [4]could meet / meet for a quick breakfast at The Coffee Pot at 9.00. Phone or send me a quick email, OK?

Sofia

**2** Match 1–5 with a–e.

1 ☐ We can't get to the airport on time, so
2 ☐ It's raining hard, so
3 ☐ They haven't prepared for the exam, so
4 ☐ We're playing really well today and
5 ☐ We've missed the bus and

a they're going to get wet.
b they're going to fail.
c we're not going to get to work on time.
d we're going to miss our flight.
e we're going to win the match.

## Vocabulary

**3** Complete the sentences with these words.

does makes plays speaks rides uses

1 My dad always __________ golf on Saturdays.
2 Jo __________ crossword puzzles on the train to work.
3 My wife __________ sandwiches for the children's lunch.
4 Sally usually __________ her bike to school.
5 She __________ a computer a lot at work.
6 Jack __________ Arabic, but he can't read it.

**4** Complete the sentences with a suitable word.

1 I love s _ _ _ _ _ _ _ _. I'm not afraid to jump out of a plane.
2 They spent all Sunday s _ _ _ _ _ _ at the ice rink.
3 I'd love to s _ _ _ on some really big waves, like in Hawaii.
4 He'd like to c_ _ _ _ the highest mountain on every continent.
5 Tony is a real d_ _ _ _ _ _ _ _. He loves to do dangerous things.
6 We saw some amazing fish when we went s_ _ _ _-d _ _ _ _ _.

## Pronunciation

**5** Which letters *r* are *not* pronounced in British English? Underline them.

thriller director store horror actress story actor

**Check your answers on >> p.88.**

What are you going to do now?

a Nothing. I'm happy.
b Revise grammar / vocabulary / pronunciation and try again.
c Ask another student / my teacher for help.

**To revise go to ...**
**Student's Book** Review >> p.35 Grammar Bank >> p.138
**Workbook** >> pp.16–19 **www.oup.com/elt/result**

## Reading

Read these texts again.

**Workbook** >> p.20 exercise 2
**Workbook** >> p.20 exercise 4

**How confident are you?**
I can understand ...

☐ some words
☐ with help
☐ when I read again
☐ everything

## Listening

Listen to this audio again.

**Workbook** >> p.21 audio script **3S.1**

**How confident are you?**
I can understand ...

☐ some words
☐ with help
☐ when I listen again
☐ everything

## Writing

Do this writing exercise again.

**Workbook** >> p.21 exercise 10

**How confident are you?**
I can write ...

☐ with help
☐ on my own
☐ with some mistakes
☐ with no mistakes

What are you going to do now?

a Nothing. I'm happy.
b Ask my teacher for help.
c Practise my reading / listening / writing.

**To practise go to ...**
**Student's Book** >> pp.26–34
**Workbook** >> pp.20–21
**MultiRom** Listening section
**www.oup.com/elt/result**

# Unit 4 Self check

4

## Grammar

**1** Complete the sentences with the verbs in brackets. Use the present perfect.

1 __________ you __________ the cat? (feed)
2 They __________ the dog for a walk. (take)
3 Lucia __________ the bathroom. (not clean)
4 We __________ everything away in the kitchen. (put)
5 __________ you __________ the shopping today? (do)
6 Dad __________ the plants. (water)
7 I __________ some friends to come here tomorrow. (invite)

**2** Write sentences.

1 Berndt / break / his leg yesterday / and now / he / be / in hospital.
2 Kirsi / have / flu / twice this year.
3 we / not / watch / TV last night.
4 you / ever / buy / something on the Internet?
5 Roger / do / a lot of work / last week.

## Vocabulary

**3** Complete the sentences with a suitable word.

1 You wash your hair with s _ _ _ _ _ _.
2 In a hotel room, drinks are in the m_ _ _-b_ _.
3 If it is cold, you can put an extra b_ _ _ _ _ _ on your bed.
4 When you sleep, you put your head on a p_ _ _ _ _.
5 Water comes out of a t_ _.
6 You use a t_ _ _ _ to dry yourself.

**4** Complete the sentences with these words.

put fallen broken cut burnt

1 Oh no! I've __________ my glasses!
2 Yuk! I've __________ salt in my coffee.
3 Oops! The plates have __________ out of the cupboard.
4 Ouch! I've __________ my finger. Look at all the blood!
5 Uh oh! I think I've __________ the toast. Can you smell it?

## Pronunciation

**5** Write the words.

1 /ʃæm'puː/ *shampoo*
2 /flɔː/ __________
3 /'taʊəl/ __________
4 /'pɪləʊ/ __________
5 /'blæŋkɪt/ __________
6 /səʊp/ __________

**Check your answers on >> p.88.**

What are you going to do now?

a Nothing. I'm happy.
b Revise grammar / vocabulary / pronunciation and try again.
c Ask another student / my teacher for help.

**To revise go to ...**
**Student's Book** Review >> p.45 Grammar Bank >> p.139
**Workbook** >> pp.22–25 **www.oup.com/elt/result**

## Reading

Read these texts again.

**Workbook** >> p.26 exercise 1
**Workbook** >> p.27 exercise 9

**How confident are you?**
I can understand ...

☐ some words
☐ with help
☐ when I read again
☐ everything

## Listening

Listen to this audio again.

**Workbook** >> p.26 audio script **4S.1**▶

**How confident are you?**
I can understand ...

☐ some words
☐ with help
☐ when I listen again
☐ everything

## Writing

Do this writing exercise again.

**Workbook** >> p.27 exercise 16

**How confident are you?**
I can write ...

☐ with help
☐ on my own
☐ with some mistakes
☐ with no mistakes

**What are you going to do now?**

a Nothing. I'm happy.
b Ask my teacher for help.
c Practise my reading / listening / writing.

**To practise go to ...**
**Student's Book** >> pp.36–44
**Workbook** >> pp.26–27
**MultiRom** Listening section
**www.oup.com/elt/result**

# Unit 5 Self check

5

## Grammar

**1** Tick ✓ the correct sentence.

1 a ☐ We don't need the heating. Turn it off.
  b ☐ We don't need the heating. Turn off it.

2 a ☐ My feet hurt. I'm going to put off my shoes.
  b ☐ My feet hurt. I'm going to take off my shoes.

3 a ☐ I want to buy this shirt, but I'll put it on first.
  b ☐ I want to buy this shirt, but I'll try it on first.

4 a ☐ We need the lights. I'll put on them.
  b ☐ We need the lights. I'll put them on.

**2** Complete the text with these words.

mustn't don't offer must offers

**Advice for giving gifts in China**

Chinese people usually refuse a gift three times, so [1]__________ the gift again and again. If somebody [2]__________ you a gift, you [3]__________ do the same. You [4]__________ give clocks because they are connected with dying. Wrap your gift, but [5]__________ wrap it in white, black or blue: use red.

## Vocabulary

**3** Complete the sentences with a suitable word.

1 She was wearing a long black d _ _ _ _.
2 When I go jogging I wear a t _ _ _ _ _ _ _ _.
3 In the summer my girlfriend wears s _ _ _ _ _ _ on her feet.
4 I bought an expensive s _ _ _ to wear at my brother's wedding.
5 I can't go shopping for shoes today because I've got holes in my s _ _ _ _!

**4** Order the words to make sentences and questions.

1 like you these do ones ?
2 are they much how ?
3 a small bit they're .
4 a jeans looking of for I'm pair .
5 how like would pay you to ?

## Pronunciation

**5** Complete the table with these words.

neat break bread near clean head great jeans hear

| /iː/ | /e/ | /eɪ/ | /ɪə/ |
|---|---|---|---|
| | | | |

**Check your answers on >> p.88.**

What are you going to do now?

a Nothing. I'm happy.
b Revise grammar / vocabulary / pronunciation and try again.
c Ask another student / my teacher for help.

**To revise go to ...**

**Student's Book** Review >> p.55 Grammar Bank >> p.140
**Workbook** >> pp.28–31 **www.oup.com/elt/result**

## Reading

Read these texts again.

**Workbook** >> p.32 exercise 1
**Workbook** >> p.33 exercise 6

**How confident are you?**
I can understand ...

☐ some words
☐ with help
☐ when I read again
☐ everything

## Listening

Listen to this audio again.

**Workbook** >> p.32 audio script **5S.1**▶

**How confident are you?**
I can understand ...

☐ some words
☐ with help
☐ when I listen again
☐ everything

## Writing

Do this writing exercise again.

**Workbook** >> p.33 exercise 12

**How confident are you?**
I can write ...

☐ with help
☐ on my own
☐ with some mistakes
☐ with no mistakes

What are you going to do now?

a Nothing. I'm happy.
b Ask my teacher for help.
c Practise my reading / listening / writing.

**To practise go to ...**

**Student's Book** >> pp.46–54
**Workbook** >> pp.32–33
**MultiRom** Listening section
**www.oup.com/elt/result**

# Unit 6 Self check

6

## Grammar

**1** Underline the correct words.

1 You have to / don't have to pass a driving test before you can drive on your own.
2 You don't have to / mustn't use a mobile phone when you're driving.
3 You have to / don't have to stop at a red light when you're driving.
4 You don't have to / mustn't wear shorts in the car.
5 You don't have to / mustn't drink and drive.

**2** Complete the text with these words.

hurt told was passing was wearing ran was driving turned

Well, I [1]__________ home and I was on Wellington Road. I [2]__________ the sports centre when a young man [3]__________ in front of me, and well, I [4]__________ to the left and crashed into a traffic light. I [5]__________ the police immediately. I [6]__________ a seat belt, but I [7]__________ my neck.

## Vocabulary

**3** Complete the sentences to make telephone phrases.

1 Please __________ the line.
2 I'll put you __________ to an operator.
3 To speak to an operator, please __________ two.
4 Would you like to __________ a message?
5 Sorry, __________ number!
6 I called a moment ago, but I got cut __________.

**4** Tick ✓ or correct the sentences.

1 You have to stop at the pedestrian cross.
2 I've got a flat wheel.
3 We have to wait for the traffic lights.
4 You can drive much faster on the motorway.
5 Put your belt seat on!

## Pronunciation

**5** Complete the table with these words.

bought broke brought caught drove got lost saw wrote

| /ɔː/ | other sounds |
|---|---|
| | |

**Check your answers on >> p.89.**

What are you going to do now?

a Nothing. I'm happy.
b Revise grammar / vocabulary / pronunciation and try again.
c Ask another student / my teacher for help.

**To revise go to ...**
**Student's Book** Review >> p.65 Grammar Bank >> p.141
**Workbook** >> pp.34–37 **www.oup.com/elt/result**

## Reading

Read these texts again.

**Workbook** >> p.38 exercise 1
**Workbook** >> p.38 exercise 5

**How confident are you?**
I can understand ...

☐ some words
☐ with help
☐ when I read again
☐ everything

## Listening

Listen to this audio again.

**Workbook** >> p.39 audio script **6S.1**▶

**How confident are you?**
I can understand ...

☐ some words
☐ with help
☐ when I listen again
☐ everything

## Writing

Do this writing exercise again.

**Workbook** >> p.39 exercise 12

**How confident are you?**
I can write ...

☐ with help
☐ on my own
☐ with some mistakes
☐ with no mistakes

**What are you going to do now?**

a Nothing. I'm happy.
b Ask my teacher for help.
c Practise my reading / listening / writing.

**To practise go to ...**
**Student's Book** >> pp.56–64
**Workbook** >> pp.38–39
**MultiRom** Listening section
**www.oup.com/elt/result**

# Unit 7 Self check

7

## Grammar

**1** Tick ✓ or correct the sentences.

1 A mechanic is someone fixes cars.
2 A surgery is a place who you see the doctor.
3 What do you call a place where borrow money?
4 What do you call someone who works in a bank?
5 A pilot is someone who fly planes.

**2** Underline the correct words.

1 He wears a turban because / so the desert sun's very hot.
2 They don't get many visitors because / so they're excited.
3 The news is good because / so they're happy.
4 Sometimes his bike breaks down because / so he has to push it.
5 I told him to come home because / so I need to see him.

## Vocabulary

**3** Complete the sentences with these words.

uniform contract valid flexible competitive experience

1 To work as a bus driver you need a __________ driving licence.
2 This job has __________ hours because you start and finish work at different times.
3 You have to wear a __________ to work in this shop.
4 This job has a __________ salary. It pays good money.
5 We are looking for a manager with five years' __________.
6 You are working here for twelve months so we'll give you a one-year __________.

**4** Complete the sentences with a suitable word.

1 A r_ _ _ _ _ _ _ _ _ _ _ works in a hotel.
2 An artist works in a s_ _ _ _ _.
3 A s_ _ _ _ _ _ _ _ answers the phone in an office.
4 A c_ _ _ _ _ _ works in a bank.
5 A n_ _ _ _ helps doctors and looks after sick people.
6 A scientist works in a l _ _ _ _ _ _ _ _ _.

## Pronunciation

**5** Complete the table with these words.

own long want won't boss show not gone note no

| /ɒ/ | /əʊ/ |
|---|---|
| | |

**Check your answers on >> p.89.**

What are you going to do now?

a Nothing. I'm happy.
b Revise grammar / vocabulary / pronunciation and try again.
c Ask another student / my teacher for help.

**To revise go to ...**

**Student's Book** Review >> p.75 Grammar Bank >> p.142
**Workbook** >> pp.40–43 **www.oup.com/elt/result**

## Reading

Read these texts again.

**Workbook** >> p.44 exercise 2
**Workbook** >> p.45 exercise 10

**How confident are you?**
I can understand ...

☐ some words
☐ with help
☐ when I read again
☐ everything

## Listening

Listen to this audio again.

**Workbook** >> p.44 audio script **7S.1**▶

**How confident are you?**
I can understand ...

☐ some words
☐ with help
☐ when I listen again
☐ everything

## Writing

Do this writing exercise again.

**Workbook** >> p.45 exercise 15

**How confident are you?**
I can write ...

☐ with help
☐ on my own
☐ with some mistakes
☐ with no mistakes

What are you going to do now?

a Nothing. I'm happy.
b Ask my teacher for help.
c Practise my reading / listening / writing.

**To practise go to ...**

**Student's Book** >> pp.66–74
**Workbook** >> pp.44–45
**MultiRom** Listening section
**www.oup.com/elt/result**

# Unit 8 Self check

## Grammar

**1** Tick ✓ the correct sentence.

1 a ☐ Where is her laptop?
  b ☐ Where is hers laptop?

2 a ☐ It's not your book. It's our.
  b ☐ It's not your book. It's ours.

3 a ☐ This isn't mine. I think it's your's.
  b ☐ This isn't mine. I think it's yours.

4 a ☐ Their car was red.
  b ☐ There car was red.

**2** Correct the sentences. The mistake is underlined.

1 My mum wont shout at me any more.
2 In the future, pets will able to talk to us.
3 Everyone will carries a mobile phone.
4 Will go you to the party tonight?

## Vocabulary

**3** Complete the sentences with suitable words.

1 A drinks can is made of m__________.
2 He's a carpenter so he works with w__________.
3 A window is made of g__________.
4 Be careful with those tea cups. They're c__________, so they could break.
5 A baby bottle is made of p__________.

**4** Complete the text with these words.

contacts email virus subject attachment

I opened an email this morning. I didn't know who sent it and the [1]__________ was just 'Good News!'. It had an [2]__________ called 'Message from a friend'. I opened it without thinking and it was a [3]__________. I think it went into my address book and sent an [4]__________ to all my [5]__________.

## Pronunciation

**5** Match 1–5 with a–e.

| | |
|---|---|
| 1 ☐ you'll | a /ʃiːl/ |
| 2 ☐ they'll | b /aɪl/ |
| 3 ☐ it'll | c /juːl/ |
| 4 ☐ she'll | d /ɪtl/ |
| 5 ☐ I'll | e /ðeɪl/ |

**Check your answers on >> p.89.**

What are you going to do now?

a Nothing. I'm happy.
b Revise grammar / vocabulary / pronunciation and try again.
c Ask another student / my teacher for help.

**To revise go to ...**
**Student's Book** Review >> p.85 Grammar Bank >> p.143
**Workbook** >> pp.46–49 **www.oup.com/elt/result**

## Reading

Read these texts again.

**Workbook** >> p.50 exercise 2
**Workbook** >> p.51 exercise 7

**How confident are you?**
I can understand ...

☐ some words
☐ with help
☐ when I read again
☐ everything

## Listening

Listen to this audio again.

**Workbook** >> p.50 audio script **8S.1**▶

**How confident are you?**
I can understand ...

☐ some words
☐ with help
☐ when I listen again
☐ everything

## Writing

Do this writing exercise again.

**Workbook** >> p.51 exercise 11

**How confident are you?**
I can write ...

☐ with help
☐ on my own
☐ with some mistakes
☐ with no mistakes

**What are you going to do now?**

a Nothing. I'm happy.
b Ask my teacher for help.
c Practise my reading / listening / writing.

**To practise go to ...**
**Student's Book** >> pp.76–84
**Workbook** >> pp.50–51
**MultiRom** Listening section
**www.oup.com/elt/result**

# Unit 9 Self check

9

## Grammar

**1** Complete the sentences with these words.

a few   a little   none   a lot   isn't much   aren't many

1 There __________ sugar in this coffee. I like it sweeter.
2 Can I have __________ milk in my tea?
3 There __________ olives in the salad. Can I have some more?
4 We've got __________ tomatoes in the fridge – two or three.
5 He's getting fat because he eats __________ of crisps.
6 'Is there any meat in this?' 'No, there's __________.'

**2** Underline the correct words.

If you go to Cabo Verde, you [1]should to / should try the seafood. But you [2]should / shouldn't drink water from the tap because you could get ill. You [3]should / mustn't buy bottled water instead. The traditional drink is *grogue*. This is an alcoholic drink and it's very strong, so you [4]musn't / mustn't drink a lot.

## Vocabulary

**3** Correct the spelling of one word in each sentence.

1 It's best to rost the meat for two hours.
2 Daria normally eats scambled eggs for breakfast.
3 We need some gratted cheese on the potatoes.
4 Don't put the salad on the babecue!
5 Gril the fish for ten minutes.

**4** Tick ✓ or correct the sentences.

1 We have to make the washing up.
2 I'm tired. Let's have a break.
3 I hate making exercise. I'd rather watch TV.
4 If you do an effort, you'll pass the exam.
5 They made a mess when they worked in the garage.

## Pronunciation

**5** Tick ✓ the sentences where you can hear the /t/ in *shouldn't*.

1 You shouldn't work too hard.
2 You shouldn't eat a lot of sweets.
3 You shouldn't put sugar on your breakfast cereal.
4 You shouldn't stay out late every night.
5 You shouldn't open that box of chocolates!

**Check your answers on >> p.89.**

**What are you going to do now?**

a Nothing. I'm happy.
b Revise grammar / vocabulary / pronunciation and try again.
c Ask another student / my teacher for help.

**To revise go to ...**
**Student's Book** Review >> p.95   Grammar Bank >> p.144
**Workbook** >> pp.52–55   **www.oup.com/elt/result**

## Reading

Read these texts again.

**Workbook** >> p.56 exercise 2
**Workbook** >> p.56 exercise 3

**How confident are you?**
I can understand ...

☐ some words
☐ with help
☐ when I read again
☐ everything

## Listening

Listen to this audio again.

**Workbook** >> p.57 audio script **9S.1**▶

**How confident are you?**
I can understand ...

☐ some words
☐ with help
☐ when I listen again
☐ everything

## Writing

Do this writing exercise again.

**Workbook** >> p.57 exercise 10

**How confident are you?**
I can write ...

☐ with help
☐ on my own
☐ with some mistakes
☐ with no mistakes

**What are you going to do now?**

a Nothing. I'm happy.
b Ask my teacher for help.
c Practise my reading / listening / writing.

**To practise go to ...**
**Student's Book** >> pp.86–94
**Workbook** >> pp.56–57
**MultiRom** Listening section
**www.oup.com/elt/result**

# Unit 10 Self check

10

## Grammar

**1** Underline the correct words.

When I was in Turkey, I [1]took / have taken a ferry across to Rhodes. I [2]stayed / have stayed there for a week and then I [3]flew / have flown home. I [4]was / have been back for three weeks now. It [5]was / has been cold and wet since I got home and I [6]lost / have lost my suntan already.

**2** Tick ✓ or correct the sentences.

1 My grandma was from Mallorca, so we use to go there a lot.
2 She used to live in a small house on the beach.
3 We used to go to Ibiza once, in 1986.
4 The plane was expensive, so we used to going by car.
5 I used to like swimming in the sea.

## Vocabulary

**3** Correct the sentences. The mistake is underlined.

1 Fowey is a thirty-minutes drive from the beaches in Newquay.
2 Fowey is at Cornwall's south coast.
3 I live in a village in a small island.
4 Zermatt is a town at the Alps.
5 The beach is a short journey on feet.
6 Central station is only a short ride bus from here.

**4** Complete the sentences with these words.

check customs duty departure control board

1 Ben changed some money before he went through passport ________.
2 I'm going to buy a watch in the ________-free shop.
3 All passengers please go to ________ gate 17.
4 You have two big suitcases and you need to ________ them in.
5 The first people to ________ the plane are families with small children.
6 ________ can look in your bag to see if you are carrying anything illegal.

## Pronunciation

**5** Decide how *used* is pronounced. Write *A* for /juːzd/ or *B* for /juːst/.

1 ☐ I used your telephone this morning.
2 ☐ We used to live in Stockholm.
3 ☐ They used a different computer program.
4 ☐ He said he used to be a musician.

**Check your answers on >> p.89.**

What are you going to do now?

a Nothing. I'm happy.
b Revise grammar / vocabulary / pronunciation and try again.
c Ask another student / my teacher for help.

**To revise go to ...**
**Student's Book** Review >> p.105 Grammar Bank >> p.145
**Workbook** >> pp.58–61 **www.oup.com/elt/result**

## Reading

Read these texts again.

**Workbook** >> p.62 exercise 1
**Workbook** >> p.62 exercise 3

**How confident are you?**
I can understand ...

☐ some words
☐ with help
☐ when I read again
☐ everything

## Listening

Listen to this audio again.

**Workbook** >> p.63 audio script **10S.1**

**How confident are you?**
I can understand ...

☐ some words
☐ with help
☐ when I listen again
☐ everything

## Writing

Do this writing exercise again.

**Workbook** >> p.63 exercise 12

**How confident are you?**
I can write ...

☐ with help
☐ on my own
☐ with some mistakes
☐ with no mistakes

What are you going to do now?

a Nothing. I'm happy.
b Ask my teacher for help.
c Practise my reading / listening / writing.

**To practise go to ...**
**Student's Book** >> pp.96–104
**Workbook** >> pp.62–63
**MultiRom** Listening section
**www.oup.com/elt/result**

# Unit 11 Self check

11

## Grammar

**1** Underline the correct words.

1 That man over there is looking / looks at me.
2 Everyone is seeming / seems tired today.
3 I'm not understanding / I don't understand this exercise.
4 I think everyone has enjoyed your presentation. They are all smiling / all smile.
5 I'm not liking / I don't like opera.
6 John has come to see you. He is standing / stands outside.

**2** Tick ✓ or correct the sentences.

1 His hair was shaved off the top of his head.
2 Veins and spots were paint on his skin.
3 The shape of his nose was change.
4 Contact lenses was put in his eyes.
5 The film was given an Oscar for best make-up.

## Vocabulary

**3** Correct the spelling of the words in the sentences.

1 I feel terrible. I've got a temprature.
2 He has a really bad cought.
3 He can't eat because he has a soar throat.
4 Lars went to the dentist with teethache.
5 Katja has been in bed with a feber.
6 I got backake because I worked on the computer too long.

**4** Complete the sentences with suitable words.

1 He was wearing a tie around his n__________.
2 In lots of countries, friends kiss each other on the c__________.
3 Wear a hat, or you'll get cold e__________.
4 A baby's s__________ is so soft!
5 Careful! The coffee's hot. You'll burn your l__________.

## Pronunciation

**5** Read the sentences aloud. Complete the table with the underlined words.

1 We have a problem with the computer.
2 Work together and compare your answers.
3 I've cut my finger.
4 Don't forget your passport!
5 They pretend to like her singing.

| ●• | •● |
|---|---|
| | |

**Check your answers on >> p.90.**

**What are you going to do now?**

a Nothing. I'm happy.
b Revise grammar / vocabulary / pronunciation and try again.
c Ask another student / my teacher for help.

**To revise go to ...**

**Student's Book** Review >> p.115 Grammar Bank >> p.146
**Workbook** >> pp.64–67 **www.oup.com/elt/result**

## Reading

Read these texts again.

**Workbook** >> p.68 exercise 1
**Workbook** >> p.68 exercise 4

**How confident are you?**
I can understand ...

☐ some words
☐ with help
☐ when I read again
☐ everything

## Listening

Listen to this audio again.

**Workbook** >> p.69 audio script **11S.1**▸

**How confident are you?**
I can understand ...

☐ some words
☐ with help
☐ when I listen again
☐ everything

## Writing

Do this writing exercise again.

**Workbook** >> p.69 exercise 11

**How confident are you?**
I can write ...

☐ with help
☐ on my own
☐ with some mistakes
☐ with no mistakes

**What are you going to do now?**

a Nothing. I'm happy.
b Ask my teacher for help.
c Practise my reading / listening / writing.

**To practise go to ...**

**Student's Book** >> pp.106–114
**Workbook** >> pp.68–69
**MultiRom** Listening section
**www.oup.com/elt/result**

# Pronunciation

| verb | past simple | past participle |
|---|---|---|
| be | was | been |
| | were | |
| break | broke | broken |
| buy | bought /bɔːt/ | bought /bɔːt/ |
| can | could /kʊd/ | been able to |
| come | came | come |
| cut | cut | cut |
| do | did | done |
| draw | drew | drawn |
| drink | drank | drunk |
| drive | drove | driven /'drɪvn/ |
| eat | ate | eaten |
| find | found | found |
| forget | forgot | forgotten |
| get | got | got |
| give | gave | given |
| go | went | gone |
| | | been |
| have | had | had |
| hear | heard /hɜːd/ | heard /hɜːd/ |
| know | knew /njuː/ | known |
| learn | learnt | learnt |
| | learned | learned |
| leave | left | left |
| lose | lost | lost |

| verb | past simple | past participle |
|---|---|---|
| make | made | made |
| meet | met | met |
| put | put /pʊt/ | put /pʊt/ |
| read | read /red/ | read /red/ |
| ring | rang | rung |
| run | ran | run |
| say | said /sed/ | said /sed/ |
| see | saw /sɔː/ | seen |
| sell | sold | sold |
| send | sent | sent |
| sing | sang | sung |
| sit | sat | sat |
| sleep | slept | slept |
| speak | spoke | spoken |
| spend | spent | spent |
| stand | stood /stʊd/ | stood /stʊd/ |
| swim | swam | swum |
| take | took /tʊk/ | taken |
| tell | told | told |
| think | thought /θɔːt/ | thought /θɔːt/ |
| understand | understood | understood |
| wake up | woke up | woken up |
| wear | wore | worn |
| write | wrote | written /'rɪtn/ |

**« Look at the verb column. Cover the past simple and past partciple columns and test yourself.**

OXFORD
UNIVERSITY PRESS
Great Clarendon Street, Oxford OX2 6DP
Oxford University Press is a department of the University of Oxford. It furthers the University's objective of excellence in research, scholarship, and education by publishing worldwide in
Oxford New York
Auckland Cape Town Dar es Salaam Hong Kong Karachi Kuala Lumpur Madrid Melbourne Mexico City Nairobi New Delhi Shanghai Taipei Toronto
With offices in
Argentina Austria Brazil Chile Czech Republic France Greece Guatemala Hungary Italy Japan Poland Portugal Singapore South Korea Switzerland Thailand Turkey Ukraine Vietnam



First published 2008
2012 2011 2010 2009 2008
10 9 8 7 6 5 4 3 2 1



ISBN: 978 0 19 430487 0

Printed in Europe

ACKNOWLEDGEMENTS

*Illustrations by*: David Atkinson p10 (map); Jo Bird p65; Mark Duffin pp14, 31, 47, 50, 58, 69 (man on bicycle); Pamela Goodchild (represented by Bl Kearley) p27; Andy Hammond pp24, 46; Phil Hankinson pp7, 34, 64; Ben Hasler (represented by NB Illustration) pp19, 39, 62; Joanna Kerr pp13, 28 (clothes), 52; George Onions pp16, 28 (man), 29, 53; Gavin Reece pp32, 73; Mark Ruffle pp10 (icons), 56; Harry Venning pp23. 69 (thieves); Terry Wong (represented by Anna Goodson management) pp8, 37, 54;

*The publishers would like to thank the following for permission to reproduce photographs*: Alamy Images pp11 (Hecho/Michelle Chaplow), 11 (lighthouse/South West Images Scotland), 14 (temple/Chuck Place), 16 (swimmer), 20 (roller-skates/D.Hurst), 25 (tourists watching volcano/Lyndon Giffard), 30 (shoe-shop), 33 (fish and chips/Charlotte Wiig), 36 (currency/vario images GmbH & Co.KG), 38 (Fernando Alonso/Howard Sayer), 43 (football fans/Paul Thompson Images), 44 (policeman/Andrew Holt), 57 (English breakfast/Images Etc Ltd), 57 (wine and cheese/Chris Fredriksson), 64 (woman with headache/Profimedia International s.r.o.); Bridgeman Art Library Ltd p67 (Page from the Charter of Kelso Abbey with an illuminated initial depicting King David I (1084–1153) and his grandson Malcolm IV (1141–65) 1159 (vellum), English School, (12th century)/Private Collection,); Corbis p20 (The Constant Gardner filmstill/Jaap Buitendijk/Focus Features/Bureau L.A. Collection); Getty Images pp4 (John Wayne/Hulton Archive), 5 (senior man/DreamPictures/The Image Bank), 9 (violinist/Piere Desrosiers/First Light), 13 (Matsumoto Castle/Gavin Hellier/The Image Bank), 18 (car breakdown/Silvia Otte/Photonica), 25 (Shakira/IML Image Group/WireImage), 30 (shoe shopping/Marcus Mok/Asia Images), 32 (model/Topic/WireImage), 42 (Natural History Museum/Rex Butcher/Stone), 44 (Brazilian Prime Minister Luiz Inacio Lula da Silva/John Thys/AFP), 44 (classroom/Michael Wildsmith/Taxi), 44 (father/Elie Bernager/Stone), 48 (colleagues/Marc Romanelli/The Image Bank), 55 (dinner/David Sacks/Stone), 59 (airplane/Tom Tracy/Taxi), 63 (safari/Theo Allofs/Stone), 66 (woman/Stock4B), 71 (Brazilian festival/Peter Adams/The Image Bank), 72 (rock climbers/Johner Images); Kobal Collection pp20 (*The Black Dahlia* film still/Universal), 21 (*Sunshine* film poster/Fox Searchlight); Moviestore Collection p20 (*Pirates of the Caribbean: Dead Man's Chest* (2006)/Disney); OUP pp6 (police interview/Chris King), 20 (ice skates/Photodisc), 53 (eggs/Photodisc); PunchStock pp9 (family/Blend Images), 15 (New Zealand/Photographer's Choice), 16 (surfer/Radius Images), 16 (skier/Digital Vision), 17 (playing piano/Blend Images), 20 (rollerblades/Photodisc), 31 (backpacker/BananaStock), 33 (restaurant/Image Source), 45 (trawlerman/Digital Vision), 47 (strawberries/Stockbyte), 48 (petrol/Photographer's Choice), 49 (typing/Image Source), 52 (coffee/Tetra Images), 57 (sandwich/Corbis), 60 (family/Brand X Pictures), 70 (airport/Glow Images).